Quality

Bird Care
and Training

An Owner's Guide To

A HAPPY HEALTHY PET

Howell Book House

Howell Book House
A Simon & Schuster Macmillan Company
1633 Broadway
New York, NY 10019

Macmillan Publishing books may be purchased for business or sales promotional use. For information please write: Special Markets Department, Macmillan Publishing USA, 1633 Broadway, New York, NY 10019.

Library of Congress Cataloging-in-Publication Data
Higdon, Pamela Leis.
Bird care and training: an owner's guide to a happy, healthy pet / Pamela Leis Higdon.
p. cm.
ISBN 0-87605227-8   2 Birds as pests - Jan let
1. Bird care and training.   I. Title.   II. Series.
SF461.H54   1998
636.6'8—dc21   98-9667
                CIP

Manufactured in the United States of America
10 9 8 7 6 5 4 3 2 1

Series Director: Amanda Pisani
Series Assistant Director: Jennifer Liberts
Book Design by Michele Laseau
Cover Design by Iris Jeromnimon
Illustration: Ryan Oldfather
Photography:
  Front cover by Eric Ilasenko
  Back cover by Joan Balzarini
Joan Balzarini: 7, 8, 10, 12, 13, 14, 19, 20, 29, 31, 33, 38, 44, 45, 52, 55, 60, 68, 69, 98–99, 109
Sherry Lee Harris: 9, 22, 36, 37, 46, 48, 53, 56, 58
Eric Ilasenko: 2–3, 63, 64, 67, 70, 71, 74, 76, 80, 82, 84, 85, 87, 88, 91, 92, 95, 96, 100, 101, 102, 106, 108, 111, 113, 115, 117, 118, 120, 122
Cheryl Primeau: 16, 50, 78, 79
J. A. Rach: 86
David Shulman: 5, 28
Bob Schwartz: 42–43, 62, 75, 83
Faith Uridel: 17, 34, 35, 116
Production Team: Clint Lahnen, Stephanie Mohler, Angel Perez, Dennis Sheehan, Terri Sheehan

Contents

About
Your

part one

New

Pet

External Features of a Bird

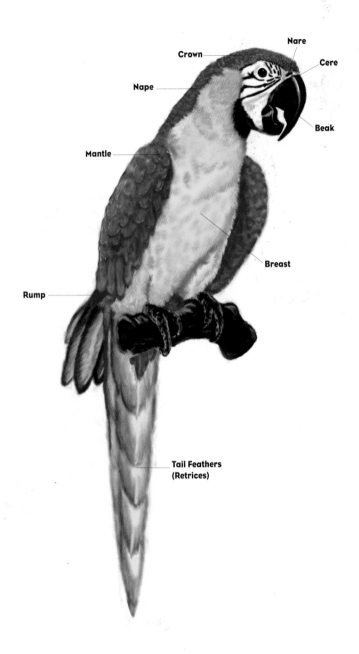

Crown

Nape

Nare

Cere

Beak

Mantle

Breast

Rump

Tail Feathers
(Retrices)

chapter 1

Bird
Ancestry

*Keep a green tree in your heart and
perhaps the singing bird will come.*
—Chinese Proverb

Congratulations on your new bird.
Your pet is sure to bring a great
deal of joy into your home. People
love birds for many reasons, including their lovely feathers, singing
and/or talking abilities and, perhaps most of all, because they are
so different from other animal
species.

You might be able to trace your
interest in birds back to childhood.
Perhaps a beloved relative had one
when you were younger. Maybe birds began to appeal to you when
you saw wild birds fly or heard the song of a bird as you played
outside.

5

Origins of Birds

Human interest in birds extends back centuries, but birds were alive long before even the first primitive humans appeared on earth. When dinosaurs ruled the land during the Jurassic Period, birds began to dominate the air. Although flying reptiles had begun to develop thirty-five million years before birds appeared, lighter, feathered birds would ultimately rule the skies.

Today, we believe that the *Archaeopteryx lithographica* was the first feathered bird. The first complete fossil record of the *Archaeopteryx* was found in Solnhofen, Germany. It was dated from the Jurassic period. Unfortunately, we have no idea of whether those birds vocalized or what color they were.

Another early bird that is remarkably similar to the *Archaeopteryx* was found not long ago in China. It dates from approximately the same time period and has been named *Confusciusornis*. Both animals had wing claws, but the *Archaeopteryx* had teeth like modern birds. The *Confusciusornis* did not have teeth.

By studying fossils, paleontologists have learned that the first true birds lived about 140 million years ago in cycad forests and were about the size of a present-day crow. Cycads are tropical and semi-tropical cone-bearing plants that are similar to palm trees.

WHAT ARE TRUE BIRDS?

True birds are considered animals with feathers that fly and have no teeth or claws on or near the tips of their wings. Flying reptiles, including the *Rhamphorhynchus* and the *Pteranodon*, had teeth, claws near the tips of the wings and no feathers. The *Archaeopteryx* is considered a transition to true birds, more like those we know today and less like reptiles, because it had feathers but it still had teeth and claws at the tips of its wings.

Because bird bones are lightweight or hollow (which allows for flight), they did not preserve well as fossils. Feathers of prehistoric birds were equally fragile. As a result, we don't have a detailed fossil record of all the bird species that we believe may have developed between the *Archaeopteryx* and birds that live today, but as more fossils are discovered, our understanding about birds and their natural adaptation through the centuries expands.

We do believe now that some modern birds, such as loons, petrels, albatrosses, ducks, gulls and shore birds, were alive sixty-five million years ago. Amazingly, most of the bird species we are familiar with today appeared on earth at least thirty-five million years ago, including Parrots, songbirds, owls, penguins, fowl, Doves and crows. Fortunately for us, some birds that were alive during that time period are extinct. The *Phororhachids* would have been especially difficult to live with. These birds were flightless, but at about 9 feet tall, their huge, sharp beaks and claws, coupled with their speed and agility, made them menacing predators. Scientists believe that these birds were the dominant carnivorous predators of South America, and possibly more tropical parts of North America, during the Cenozoic Period. During the Eocene Period, a similar flightless, predatory bird, the *Diatrymidae*, was a dominant species in North America and Europe. Present-day cranes, rails and coots are likely ancestors of those carnivorous birds.

Most of the bird species we are familiar with today appeared on earth at least thiry-five million years ago!

As birds developed ways to survive, such as the ability to maneuver on the ground as well as in the air, they gradually became quite successful at finding food and claiming territories in which to live and hunt. In addition, their high rate of metabolism and warm-blooded natures gave them an edge over other animals, especially reptiles.

Birds Today

As the number of true birds increased, they competed more successfully for food, and flying reptiles eventually died out. Today, about 8,500 species of birds live all over the earth, although their numbers are in constant decline because of the loss of habitat and the vast numbers of wild birds captured for sale as pets. Birds are a successful species, though; by comparison, there are only about 4,000 species of mammals.

WHEN DID BIRDS BECOME PETS?

Our interest in keeping birds as pets has its roots in ancient history. We know from literature and art that songbirds were kept by Chinese emperors and noble families many centuries ago. The Pekin Robin, or nigh-

Alexander the Great may have been one of the first to introduce Parrots to Europe.

tingale, is still a popular pet among those who value the beauty of this small bird's form, coloring and song. We also know that birds were kept in ancient cultures of the Middle East, where falcons are still prized and used for hunting. Beyond these general guidelines, it is difficult to pinpoint the exact time bird keeping began.

It is believed by many that Alexander the Great may have been among the first to bring tame Parrots to Europe from Asia. The Alexandrine Parakeet (*Psittacula cyanocephala*) is named after this legendary warrior. Roman nobility kept Parrots as a sign of status. Later, when European explorers began extending their searches for new and interesting treasures farther and farther abroad, they sent home many birds, especially during the 15th and 16th centuries. Only the wealthy could afford to keep imported birds, though.

In the 18th century, Duc de Nivernais, from France, wrote about his Finch aviary, a unique way to house birds in that day and age. Most birds had previously been kept in tiny cages or chained to perches. His aviary comprised a large, fine net that covered a small wooded area near his home. In 1889, Arthur Butler wrote *Foreign Finches in Captivity*. This book described Australian Finches and ways to keep them.

As transportation became more efficient, wild birds were captured for keeping in distant parts of the world. It became possible to buy a bird whose natural habitat was continents away.

In the United States, bird keeping was quite popular in the '50s and early '60s. It was fairly easy to find most South American birds, as well as some African species such as Lovebirds and African Grey Parrots. Budgerigars and Cockatiels from Australia were imported in large numbers, as well as some Finches and Cockatoos.

Domestically bred birds tend to be healthier than those that are imported.

PRESERVATION EFFORTS

Fortunately for bird lovers the world over, people are beginning to understand the importance of preserving wild-bird species. Wanton harvesting of wild-bird populations has largely stopped because of international laws prohibiting their export or import. The airline industry has also helped by refusing to carry birds that are protected by such laws. As late as the mid-1980s, it was possible to contact dealers in Singapore, for example, and order any kind of bird in the world, endangered or not. If a person was willing to pay the price, the bird could be had. Today, most pet-bird species that are available in North America and Europe were bred domestically. This not only helps to ensure that pet owners will get a healthy bird, it also helps to guarantee that species favored by humans as pets will not become extinct.

Importation Restrictions

The free-for-all importation of wild-caught birds came to a screeching halt in the early '70s when Newcastle Disease, carried by wild birds, began to devastate the domestic poultry industry, especially in southern California. Newcastle Disease is species specific: Humans cannot contract this disease from birds. Illegally imported birds were believed to be the most important cause of the spread of the disease in North America during that time, and during a later outbreak in the '90s. Individual American states, responsible for the enforcement of their own importation laws, began to actively do so. Illegally imported birds were tracked down and euthanized. Federal quarantine laws were also more stringently enforced, and fewer wild-caught birds were imported for the pet trade than had been previously.

Restricting the import of wild-caught birds helped reduce the spread of disease in North America.

During the '80s, people began to recognize another important problem with wild-caught birds. Many species were being devastated all over the world due to poor handling. Of the thousands of any species caught, shipped to central holding places and then on to Asia, Europe or North America, only a few survived long enough to make it to pet stores, breeding facilities or homes.

Protective Laws

In 1992, the Convention on International Trade in Endangered Animals (CITES) met in Japan. Agreements were drawn up to limit the exportation and importation of birds. Among bird lovers at that time there was a great deal of concern over the future of bird keeping. Fortunately, most of those fears have proven to be unfounded. The knowledge that it would no longer be easy to buy inexpensive imported birds prompted aviculturists to step up efforts to breed birds.

The restrictive CITES laws also encouraged people to begin to look at and appreciate the positive aspects of breeding exotic birds domestically; such birds often make better pets because they have been either hand-fed or have been around humans enough that they are unafraid of them. These birds are also more likely to be healthy than are imported birds. An important benefit of domestic breeding has been the restoration of several species that had teetered on the brink of extinction.

chapter 2

The
Physical
Bird

Today, there are more than 8,500 species of birds all over the earth. Although they come in diverse colors, sizes and shapes, they all have certain characteristics in common.

Feathers

All birds have feathers, and they are the only animals that have them. Feathers are outgrowths of the skin, similar to hair in humans. Their main functions are to act as insulation, waterproofing and, in most birds, to aid in flight. Birds also use feathers in courtship rituals and to display territorial aggression. Feathers act as camouflage, helping birds hide from their predators.

FEATHER COLOR

Color is one of the first things you will notice about your bird. No matter which species you chose, she will have lovely feathers in an interesting pattern of colors. African Greys are some-times referred to as "just gray," but are valued because of their talking abilities. Under careful scrutiny, though, you can see that each dark-gray feather on her chest, head and neck is edged in a delicate shade of lighter gray. The longer you examine this bird, or any other, the more subtle color shadings you will notice.

A Sulfur-Crested Cockatoo might appear at first to be pure white with a yellow crest on her head. However, she has a suffusion of the palest yellow in the sheer feathers that cover her ears, and yellow in a slightly darker hue that tints the underside of her wings.

Some color is decided by pigments within the feathers. Green, for example, is thought to be a combination of blue and yellow pigments. You can tell if a feather color is pigment based if it does not change color when you view it in natural light from a different angle.

The feathers of a healthy bird will be shiny and vibrant.

Other colors are caused by the way in which light reflects from the feather's surface. White feathers reflect all light and appear white, while black feathers absorb all light and appear black.

A healthy bird's feathers will have a sheen. When the bird is sick, her feathers may look dull. Some veterinarians believe this loss of iridescence is due to the inability of sick birds to fully utilize nutrients.

How Color Helps Birds

A bird's feather color is not simply decorative; color serves birds well in many capacities. A peacock, for instance, spreads his lovely tail in front of a female that he hopes to entice. If he is healthy, his tail feathers are a lush fan of iridescent blues and greens that may encourage the female to mate with him. In most

13

animal species, if the female has a choice, she will mate with the healthiest male. This helps to ensure the survival of the species by passing along the best genes to her offspring. This is not, as far as we know, a conscious decision a female bird makes; it is believed to be instinctive.

The male Eclectus' green feathers help him to blend in with the forest when he is in search of food.

Birds with crests use these feathers to show aggression, anger, fear or excitement. When a Cockatoo throws up her orange, pink or yellow crest, back away until you figure out what feeling has caused her to do so. As you get to know your bird, you will learn the ways in which she uses her feathers to show a variety of feelings.

Camouflage   Color camouflage is one of the most interesting ways in which feathers play a part in a bird's everyday life. Eclectus Parrots fooled aviculturists for many years. The male of all the Eclectus subspecies is green with a bit of red under his wings. His flight feathers, on his wings, are black on the underside. The ground color for all females is a deep red. Subspecies differ with the addition on some of blue or violet. You can read avicultural musings on why the female of this species is so strikingly colored, when females of most species are dull greens, grays and browns that blend in with plants to camouflage them from predators.

The red coloring of the female Eclectus seems all the more unusual when you consider that survival of the females is of utmost importance to the survival of a species. It takes many females and only a few males to produce enough offspring to ensure that a species continues.

In Eclectus' natural habitat, it becomes clear that the coloring of both sexes does help camouflage them well. Males do all of the searching for food by flying among the tree-top canopy. Their green coloring blends in well with the forest, and the black feathers under their wings help to hide them in the shadows as they fly. A female Eclectus stays in her nest hole nearly all the time. Her dark-red feathers help her blend into the shadows of the deep, dim hole. It's difficult to see a female Eclectus in her nest hole—or in a nest box for that matter.

About Your Bird's Coloring

Find out where your bird's species originated, where wild birds of that species roost and how they eat; then you can begin to see the connection. Eclectus rarely come to ground for food, so they need to match the upper foliage of the forest canopy. Budgies are ground birds, and the green, black and yellow stripes of a wild Budgie blend well with the seedlings they eat on the ground. The slightly irregular stripes also break up the outline of their bodies, helping to make them less visible to predators.

COLOR AND CAMOUFLAGE

I failed to understand the strong association between color and camouflage until I viewed a variety of Parrots in the wild. My Cockatoo, Gandalf, is white with a bright-yellow crest. I wondered how that combination could hide one wild bird much less a flock—until I began looking for Cockatoos in Australia. A whole flock of Sulfur-Crested Cockatoos like Gandalf was difficult to see in trees. The sun is bright and the Cockatoos' white and yellow feathers seem to become a part of the shadow play created by the leaves of the trees these birds favor as roosts. They were especially difficult to find in eucalyptus trees. I found that I could always hear these birds long before I could see them.

While I worked for several avian magazines, a subscriber sent in a photo of her Blue Fronted Amazon perched in her backyard tree. At first glance the bird was not apparent—perfect camouflage.

FEATHER TYPES

Look carefully at your bird's feathers, and you will find a lot to fascinate you. All feathers are not alike. Certain feathers grow on specific parts of a bird's body, each fulfilling a certain function. Feathers grow in rows, unlike human hair that grows randomly. This is most obvious on chicks that have only down concealing the neat rows of feather follicles.

Contour Feathers

Run your hands over the outline of your bird's body, including the wings and tail. As your hands move from head to tail down your bird's body, you are feeling the contour feathers. They are asymmetrical and smooth,

streamlining your bird's body so that air flows smoothly over it in flight.

Now run your hand gently over your bird's abdomen and back (if she will allow it). You are feeling a slightly different kind of contour feather, also called a body feather. Compare several kinds of contour feathers, those over the ear holes and those on the back, for example. Those protecting your bird's ears will be more sheer than the dense feathers necessary to keep the bird warm on other parts of her body. The sheer feathers allow her to hear sounds clearly, an important survival skill. If she had feathers of similar construction all over her body, including her ears, sounds would be muffled or perhaps lost.

Coverts

Coverts are the small, asymmetrical feathers on the wings and tail that cover the base of the larger feathers, called remiges and retrices.

Remiges

Remiges are found on the wing. They are stiff and long. Gently pull one of your bird's wings away from her body. Birds have the longest wing feathers toward the tip of the wing, with gradually shorter feathers in toward the body. The longest feathers are called primary flight feathers, of which there are about ten on each wing. The shorter feathers are called secondary feathers, and each bird has about ten per wing.

As you get to know your bird and look more carefully at her feathers, you will notice subtle differences in various feathers of the same basic type.

Place two flight feathers next to each other. The feather on the leading edge of a flying bird's wing is longer than the next one, and the shape is slightly different to expedite flying. Each shape facilitates lift, allowing the bird to take off, fly, glide and land smoothly.

Retrices

Your bird's tail is made up of feathers called retrices. These are a type of flight feather and are constructed much like remiges, or wing flight feathers. These help a bird determine the direction of her flight.

Underneath the contour feathers are soft down feathers. This type of feather adds warmth through insulation; warm air is trapped between the down, which has a clingy quality, and the bird's skin. For weeks, newly hatched chicks have only down feathers to keep them warm. Their parents keep the chicks covered with their own bodies to regulate the babies' heat.

The bird's longest feathers are called primary flight feathers.

Growing Feathers

As you feel your bird's body, you may notice some prickly cylindrical shapes. These are growing feathers, or pin feathers. As the new feather begins to grow, the old feather loosens and falls out. Your bird will probably object to your touching these feathers because they are sensitive and too much pressure or pushing on the feather in the wrong direction can cause your bird great pain.

Each pin feather contains a blood supply to utilize while the feather grows. If you look carefully, you can see the blood through the semi-clear keratin feather sheath. If the feather breaks while it still has a blood source, the pin feather (also called a blood feather) will bleed. If your bird breaks a large blood feather, she is in danger of dying unless you stop the bleeding immediately. (See the wing-trimming section in chapter 6.)

When the feathers are fully grown, the blood source will recede. When there is no longer any blood in the shaft, your bird will preen it to remove the sheath covering the feather. If feathers are not in her reach, such as those on the top of her head, she will need your help to remove the sheaths. You can do this by gently grasping the feather with two fingernails and scraping off the sheath. This is not only beneficial, it will help to strengthen the bond between you and your bird.

If she will allow you to preen her feathers, she trusts you. If you do it carefully, her trust and dependence on you will grow. In the wild, preening is a flock behavior, one performed by a bird's mate.

Powder-Down Feathers

Some birds, including Cockatoos, Cockatiels and African Greys, have a special kind of feather that breaks off in little pieces to form powder. These powder-down feathers grow near the area where their legs meet their bodies. The powder helps keep their feathers clean and may help to repel water.

Another adaptation of the Eclectus is its head, neck and chest feathers, which are so fine that they look like human hair. Body and wing feathers look similar to those of other species.

Damaged Feathers

Feather condition is one way to determine your bird's overall health and well-being. Birds that are emotionally, physically or nutritionally stressed will have feathers that indicate trouble. I was hospitalized for six weeks a few years ago. During that time, my

birds did not get their normal share of attention, and
their diets suffered as well.

When new feathers grew in, one bird had narrow
yellow bands on her normally red feathers; the other
bird's white feathers had odd
spaces, forming featherless bars.
With determined care and a return
to their formerly balanced diet,
both birds recovered, but it took
about a year for their feathers to
return to normal.

Feathers can be damaged by a number of things, including dirt. It's important to offer your bird the
means and opportunity to bathe—
in plain water, not commercial
solutions.

Beaks

All birds have beaks, and the shape
of the beak can tell you a lot about
a species. Although bird beaks are used for the same
functions as human teeth and lips, they must also serve
other functions as well, such as grooming; locating,
securing and tearing food; climbing; defense; building
nests and feeding chicks.

*Although a wet
bird will appear
somewhat dishe-
veled, birds need
regular baths.*

HARD BEAKS

A beak is comprised of a mandible (lower jaw) and a
maxilla (upper jaw). Parrots have hard beaks while
other birds, such as Finches, have softer beaks. The
shape and hardness of a species' beak developed over
long periods of time and were probably most in-
fluenced by available food sources. For example, the
Parrot's hard, hooked beak is well suited to cracking
hard nuts and bones, as well as digging into fruit
and vegetables and cracking seeds. Birds that lived
near an abundance of nuts needed hard, curved
beaks to survive. Those without this kind of beak might
have died.

Soft Beaks or Bills

Finches (including Canaries) and other songbirds have softer bills, which are hard enough to crack seeds, but not hard enough to crack open nuts or bones. The cone shape of the beak allows the bird to exert a great deal of pressure on a seed, causing the shell to crack as it pushes against the bird's upper mandible.

Long Beaks

Toucans, Toucanets and Aracaris have fascinating beaks: They are long and (often) brightly colored. The beak length allows these birds to reach into nest holes to grab other birds' chicks or eggs, as well as fruit and insects. These brightly colored, stand-out beaks might seem a liability when the birds are asleep, allowing predators to spot the sleeping Toucans. In reality, a Toucan turns her beak to face her tail and tucks her beak under her wing while she sleeps; she looks like a black and white lump on a branch—an effective means of camouflage.

Parrots need hard, hooked beaks to crack nuts and seeds.

Baby Beaks

Most newly hatched chicks will have a projection on the top of the upper mandible called an egg tooth. This helps a chick break out of her egg. During this fascinating process, the chick's neck involuntarily jerks back repeatedly, which breaks the shell in a circle around the middle of the egg. Within a few weeks of hatching the egg tooth is gone; it grows out and is worn off at the tip of the beak.

A bird's beak will continue to grow at a steady rate throughout her life. Normal chewing on hardwood toys and climbing activities, as well as regular bathing and a balanced diet, will keep a healthy bird's beak in trim.

A Sensory Aid

Corpuscles found at the tips of all beaks are believed to work as sensory organs, relaying information to the bird's brain about food, perhaps temperature, consistency and taste. I've noticed that when I offer new food to a Parrot, she presents the upper mandible to me, beak closed. She will take a bit of the food, cream of wheat for instance, on the tip of her beak. She seems to be able to decide from that small amount on her beak if she will eat the food.

Birds' beaks are sensitive to heat, cold and pressure. Veterinarians have noted a pain response when too much pressure is applied to a bird's beak.

Health Concerns

A bird's beak can indicate a variety of health problems. If your bird's beak begins to grow longer than is normal, take your pet to an avian veterinarian for a thorough examination. Some pet groomers will recommend regular trimming of a bird's beak; this is not recommended by knowledgeable bird keepers, however, as it can be dangerous to your bird's health.

Color changes to a bird's beak, especially in Toucans and Lorikeets, may also indicate that a bird is ill. Such changes are most likely to be caused by poor nutrition. A change in the shape of a bird's beak can spell disaster and is a definite indication of a health problem.

One of my bird's developed beak mites several years ago. I noticed a slight change in his beak one morning, so I took him to his veterinarian that afternoon. He was cured a few days later, and the mites have never returned.

The Digestive System

A wild bird of any species expends a great deal of energy each day searching for food, protecting her territory, evading predators and hatching, as well as feeding, chicks. This activity level demands a huge amount of stamina. A bird's body temperature is high—much higher than a human's. The temperature range among bird species is 104° to 112° Fahrenheit, and maintaining this heat requires a great deal of fuel, in the form of food.

Birds use food to fuel their active lifestyle.

When a bird takes food into her mouth, she uses her tongue and the top of her upper mandible to mash, crush, hull and get it ready to swallow. Some Parrots,

but not all, can hold their food in a foot to help get the food to their mouths. Finches, Pekin Robins, Toucans, Canaries and other small birds do not hold their food in their feet. Those that do not use a foot in this way may stand on food or simply drop what they cannot bite off.

As the bird's food makes its way down her esophagus, special glands moisten it and begin to break it down for digestion. The next stop through the digestive system is the crop.

THE CROP

At the base of the bird's neck is the crop, which comprises a sac-like enlargement of the esophagus. Food collects here after it is swallowed, and is softened before moving on to the stomach. In a chick, the crop is prominent and is a good way to gauge the movement of food through her system.

Chicks eat voluminous amounts of soft food, either premasticated by the parents or formula from a syringe or spoon fed by a human caregiver. As a chick gulps the food, the crop quickly becomes distended. If the chick is healthy, the food will gradually and steadily empty into her stomach. If she is not healthy, the food sits in the crop for a long time, alerting the hand-feeder and veterinarian to health problems.

When the food gradually leaves the crop it feeds into your bird's stomach, which is divided into two parts. The proventriculus, sometimes called the true stomach, adds digestive juices to the food, which continues to break down. The second part of the stomach, sometimes referred to as the gizzard, is a muscular organ that breaks down food as it moves toward the small intestine, where the food begins to be absorbed into the bird's blood stream to provide energy for her body.

This process occurs relatively quickly, especially compared to that of mammals. A healthy bird defecates about every fifteen to twenty minutes through her cloaca, under the tail. Both urinary and fecal material are expelled from the bird's body at the same time. A bird stores food in her cloaca for only a few hours; this is an aid to flying, which would be hindered by a body heavy with waste material.

THE WASTE DISPOSAL SYSTEM

A bird's urinary system is simple, comprised of two kidneys and ureters, but no bladder or urethra such as mammals have. Urine produced in the kidneys is carried by the ureters to the cloaca and then eliminated from the body in a semi-solid form. Avian urine is a whitish color and is usually in the center of the more solid feces, which are green. These are usually referred to as droppings. They do not have an odor and are another way to tell if your bird is in good health. Watch for changes in color, shape, consistency and frequency.

The Respiratory System

Birds have the most efficient breathing system of any animal. This is necessary because of the intense oxygen requirements of flight. Each bird has a pair of lungs, as we do, but there the similarity stops. A bird's body is also filled with air sacs. When a bird breathes, she takes oxygen in through a pair of openings, or nostrils, in her cere, above the beak. The air continues through the bird's sinuses and through the throat (pharynx) to fill her air sacs, which pull and push air out of the lungs for oxygen exchange.

This adaptation also makes birds more susceptible to problems caused by airborne contaminants. Even those that might not noticeably affect you can kill your bird. For many years, miners have understood that birds can be early indicators of poisoned air. For that reason, miners, particularly in coal mines, often took a caged Canary with them deep in the mine shaft. If the Canary seemed healthy, they assumed the air was healthful. If the Canary died, miners got out of the tunnel as fast as they could; their deaths could not be far behind.

Birds are also susceptible to respiratory diseases because of the increased sensitivity of their larger breathing system.

Cardiovascular System

To carry the oxygen brought into the bird's body by her efficient respiratory system is an equally effective cardiovascular system. The four-chambered heart is large, when compared to the rest of the bird's body, and it beats faster than any mammal heart. Blood is pumped through the bird's heart at a tremendous rate, much faster than yours in even the smallest Budgie or Canary.

IT'S IN THE EYES

Watch your bird's use of her eyelids to see whom she trusts most. In my home, my birds will sit between my husband and me in the evening. After they have begun to relax, they all close the eye on the side of their heads facing me. They keep the eyelids open on the side facing Sherman; it never fails. If they are with me at my desk or at the computer, they will face me, sitting on my hand or the desk, both eyes closed. When my grandson Nicky and my daughter Kathie are here, all birds always keep both eyes open; the youngsters are full of activity and unpredictability, as far as the birds are concerned.

Sensory Organs
TASTE

We know that birds taste, but they seem to have fewer taste buds than mammals and other animals. Another difference between birds and other animals is that their taste buds are found on the roof of the mouth. As you become familiar with your bird, you will notice that she will first test a new food on the tip of her upper mandible and then use her tongue to palpitate a tiny bit of food on the inside of her mouth. After devoting considerable time to tasting the food, the bird will either accept more or reject the food.

We cannot generalize about birds' likes and dislikes in food tastes any more than we can generalize among humans. Some birds like sweet tastes, while others prefer sour or hot food. Like humans, some birds like everything. Among my three birds, one eats only sour or spicy foods, one eats only spicy food and the third will eat anything. When introducing the necessary variety into your bird's diet, you will simply have to try many foods, over and over again.

SIGHT

Birds see exceptionally well. Good vision is necessary for the survival of the species; birds must be able to spot food and potential predators from a long distance, even while in flight. We can only imagine the clarity with which they can see things from far away.

Eyes and vision are another aspect of your bird that will fascinate and amaze you. Their eyes are large compared to the size of their heads. Although birds have less mobility in their eyes than other animals, their ability to move their heads quickly 180° seems to compensate for this deficiency. Birds have three eyelids: One closes from the top to the middle of the eye, the second goes from the bottom to the middle of the eye and a third moves across the eyeball from side to side. This third eyelid zips across the bird's eyes to blink more than thirty times a minute, keeping the bird's eyes moist.

> ### A BIRD'S-EYE VIEW
>
> Sitting on the couch and looking out the window with my Cockatoo one day, I was amazed when he began shouting "Hi!" to something above us. I have excellent long-distance vision, but it took me quite a while to make out the small speck of a circling bird far above us. Gandalf can also pick out a bird of prey from so far away that I cannot see the bird's telltale shape, much less its color or other identification clues.

Birds' eyes come in various colors, but are standard by species. In some species, however, males and females have a different eye color. This feature is called sexual dimorphism, and can take many forms, such as eye color and feather color. For example, male Eclectus Parrots have orange irises, while females have yellow. Many male Cockatoo species have black irises, and females have brown or reddish brown.

About Your
New Pet

Signal of Moods

Eye color can be an important emotional signal, too. If an Amazon or an African Grey Parrot "pins" her eyes so the irises seem to enlarge, then reduce in size in succession, this indicates excitement. Until you know the bird and can use this as an aid to gauge a bird's mood, you should back away and leave the bird alone. If pressed, the bird could give you a nasty bite.

Female Eclectus Parrots are known for their temperamental natures and ferocity if challenged. This is a necessary trait; in the wild, she alone must protect her nest and chicks from all predators, including snakes and lizards much larger than she. An angry or frightened female Eclectus' pupils become quite small and the yellow irises become lighter and more prominent, something a predator looking into a nest hole would certainly see immediately. If you are confronted with a bird with any change in eye color, save yourself from injury and use discretion in approaching the bird. This is not an infallible method of avoiding harm, however; also be aware of other body language that indicates a stressed or angry bird.

Around your bird's eyes, you will see what appear to be eyelashes. These are covered with small feathers called semiplumes and serve the same function as our lashes: They help keep out dust, dirt and other small foreign objects.

WHERE ARE THEIR EARS?

Your bird's ears will fascinate you because they are so different from our own. Birds do not have ear flaps. If you look at your bird's head, behind her eyes and down a bit, you should notice that the quality of the feathers varies somewhat; they should be somewhat more sheer or farther apart. Gently rub your bird's head with your thumb near where her upper and lower mandibles join. Move your thumb in a gentle, circular pattern over the side of the skull. You will soon locate her ear, either by touch or sight.

HEARING

Birds hear well; this is a defense mechanism necessary to their survival. It is thought that birds can differentiate sounds more quickly than humans because they learn complicated song and sound patterns from each other as chicks. They are well able to tell the direction of a sound. If you call to your bird from another room, she will vocalize in answer. If she is out of her cage she may try to find you by flying or walking.

SMELL

Birds smell, but how well is a controversial subject. Vultures, of course, have a keen sense of smell to help them locate carrion. Other birds, such as songbirds, Parrots and Doves, are more likely to locate food with their superb eyesight.

I have tried to determine my birds' ability to smell, but have not come to any firm conclusions. While food cooks, one of my birds always becomes agitated, in anticipation of mealtime. Truthfully, though, I cannot tell whether her reaction is due more to my presence in the kitchen (a sure sign that a meal is forthcoming), or to the inevitable sounds of cooking. If Chinese food is delivered to our home, as soon as I open the cartons, she begins pacing, but that could still be a reaction to the sight of the food containers. This is something you can try to determine for yourself. It's a never-ending game in our home. Rosebud doesn't mind—as long as she gets her fair share of food.

Bones

Bones and the bird's skeletal system are another wonderful adaptation unique to birds that allows these animals to fly. When you think of animal bones, especially mammal bones, you may think first of their weight. If bird bones were as heavy in relationship to their size as mammal bones are to the size of mammals, birds could not fly. Many bird bones are hollow, making them light and allowing flight.

Specialized bones in the bird's body are called pneumatic bones because they contain air sacs and are part of the respiratory system. Included in this group are the humorous (long wing bone attached to the bird's body), ribs, vertebrae (neck bones), pelvis, sternum (keel bone) and sometimes the femur (upper leg bone). While such adaptations allow birds to fly and help them breathe efficiently, they also make their bones more fragile than other animals' bones. Fragile bones can break easily, and it will be up to you to help protect your bird from such injuries.

Many bird bones are fused together, a remarkable adaptation seen in bird skeletons. In human skeletons, muscles hold bones together. Muscles are heavy; fused, hollow bones form a lightweight skeleton that permits flight.

Avian skull bones are also fused, thereby making the beak more powerful. Birds have a unique neck construction that helps balance them in flight and let them turn their heads 180°, for defense, locating food and preening back and tail feathers.

THE KEEL BONE

The keel bone, or sternum, of most birds must be particularly strong to support the powerful

Due to the unique bone structure of birds' necks, they are able to turn their heads 180°.

chest muscles that sustain the movement of the flying bird's wings. This bone is the center of an airborne bird's body and the focus of the majority of her weight, including muscle tissue and bone.

While birds such as chickens, emus and ostriches do not fly, they still have strong keel bones and chest muscles, but their leg muscles and bones are also massive, which allows them to run quickly. The penguin, another flightless bird, does not run, but has developed the muscles necessary for swimming.

Feet

Birds use their feet for different things, depending on their natural location, where they live within that habitat and their survival needs, such as obtaining and eating food.

Finches, songbirds, Doves, Pigeons and chickens have three toes that point forward and one that points toward the bird's back. Finch toes are thin and delicate, perfect for grasping tiny branches. These birds do not walk so much as they hop. They are often only on the ground long enough to pick up food and fly away with it. Doves, Pigeons and chickens have better-developed foot pads and sturdier legs to support their ground-feeding behavior.

TOES

Parrots, Toucans, Toucanets, Aracaris and Touracos have two toes that point toward the front of the bird and two that point toward the back. This arrangement allows these birds to walk well on any surface, some

Birds have toes that are arranged to allow most species to climb easily.

with a waddling gait. This arrangement of toes also lets some bird species grasp food in a foot while sitting on the other foot, much as a human might handle food in a hand.

Parrots are expert climbers, because this toe/foot pattern allows them to grasp branches, tree trunks, wire cages or just about anything else that looks appealing. Birds that spend a lot of time in the water, such as geese, ducks or flamingoes, have webbed feet. This gives them an advantage when swimming because the webs push water,

moving the bird forward. Webbed feet are also an advantage on the wet shoreline where they help spread out the bird's body weight for greater support and easier walking on mud or sand. Penguins have webbed feet for swimming and walking on ice and snow.

29

Legs and feet are covered with scales. The skin is dry and flaky. Birds that live in snow, such as some northern owls, have feathers on their feet.

Skin

As you pet your bird, part her feathers to look at her skin. It is quite different from yours. A normal, healthy bird's skin is thin to the point of being sheer, and it is dry. The skin will look pink, but that is the color of the muscle below the skin, rather than the skin itself.

Birds have no sweat glands. To control her body temperature, a bird must pant rapidly, pull her feathers in close to her body and hold her wings away from her body if she is too hot. If she is too cold, she will puff out her feathers to help trap her body heat. She will also pull one foot up into her feathers to keep it warm.

A Male or a Female?

For many reasons, you may want to know the sex of your bird. Some birds are sexually dimorphic—you can easily tell males from females by looking at them. Budgies are my favorite example. Also called Parakeets in North America, male and female Budgies look alike except for their ceres: Adult female ceres are brown, and adult male Budgies have blue ceres. An immature Budgie has a lavender cere.

Gouldian Finches are a good example of sexual dimorphism manifested in the bird's feather color; the normal male has a deep-red face and crown. A band of black runs around the red, forming a kind of mask, and bordering this is a brilliant turquoise band. The back of the bird's head and her wings are a deep olive green. She has an electric-blue bib and a golden-yellow breast. The female has all of those colors in the same places, but they are quite muted. Male Zebra Finches are cute little birds with gray heads, orange beaks, rust-orange cheek patches, black stripes on the throat, white abdomens and black and white tail feathers. The females are mostly gray with orange beaks and a black stripe running vertically from each of their eyes and a black band on the sides of their beaks.

WHY LEARN YOUR BIRD'S SEX?

If you have chosen a bird from the many thousand species that are not sexually dimorphic, there are still ways to find out if you have a male or a female. Before you go further, though, you might reflect on your reason for learning your bird's sex. Some methods are necessarily dangerous, and others are expensive.

If you want to breed your pet, you will need to know the sex. Before a bird is paired for mating, she should be examined by an avian veterinarian, both internally and externally.

Learning your bird's sex can be risky and expensive, so give it a lot of thought before proceeding.

Surgical Sexing

The internal examination is done with an endoscope, which is inserted into the body cavity of an anesthetized bird, through a small incision. During the exam, the veterinarian will find either the testes of a male bird or the ovaries of a female bird. An advantage of this visual examination is that the vet can make sure the bird's reproductive system and other organs are strong enough to support reproductive activity and passing along her gene pool. This method, called surgical sexing or surgical sex determination, carries with it certain risks. Anytime you anesthetize and operate on an animal there is a chance the animal may die or fail to recover. The risk is considered minimal, but if you only want to know your pet's sex to satisfy your curiosity, choose a more passive, safer method,

31

such as DNA testing, feather sexing or fecal steroid analysis.

Fecal Steroid Analysis

In fecal steroid analysis, you collect a clean sample of a sexually mature bird's droppings and mail them to a laboratory for analysis. Analysis is determined by the presence of male or female reproductive hormones. Sexual maturity varies by species. Generally, small birds, such as Budgies, Finches and Lovebirds, mature more quickly than longer-lived, larger species, such as Macaws, Cockatoos and African Greys.

Feather Sexing

Feather sexing caused quite a stir about twelve years ago when it surfaced for use by the general public. Suddenly, a curious pet owner willing to spend the money could pull a blood feather, pack it in a special ice pack and mail it to a laboratory. Analysis of the pulp reveals the presence of either male or female chromosomes.

DNA Sexing

DNA sexing is another interesting development of the last decade. This procedure uses red blood cells to find the presence of female or male chromosomes and is relatively inexpensive. One advantage of this method is that you can have your bird's DNA fingerprint done at the same time. If your bird is lost and then recovered, this fingerprint can prove that she is yours. Before you decide to use any of these methods, discuss them with your avian veterinarian, who can guide your decision.

chapter 3

The
Emotional
Bird

Birds are complex animals with complex emotional needs. Most wild birds live in flocks. A bird's flock is his support system. He looks for and eats food with his flock. Many flocks have sophisticated systems for spotting predators and alerting each other. Some also care for each other's chicks, including those that fall out of a nest. Think of birds as extroverts—they gain energy from the active personalities and antics of their flock mates.

Flock Behavior

Flock behavior is rooted in the need for a species to survive, a basic instinct in all animals. It would be difficult for a wild bird to survive alone. Birds groom each other's feathers, for example, and while this is necessary because a bird cannot reach some of his own feathers, mutual preening is also a way to bond. Think of how good it feels to have your hair brushed or your scalp massaged and you may come close to understanding the mutual feeling flock mates or bonded pairs engender in each other.

Hand-fed birds maintain the instinctive need for flock support. This does not mean that they need to live in a large group of birds, but it does mean that you must replace that flock by loving, grooming and generally meeting your bird's needs. You must take over the flock's job of making your bird feel secure. This is not a twenty-four-hour-a-day chore, but it will require dedication, thought and planning.

Giving your bird lots of love and attention provides him with the support he would get from his flock.

Getting Acquainted

Before you bring your bird home, learn as much about his species as possible; some birds require far more active attention and interaction than others. A Moluccan Cockatoo, for example, is a high-maintenance bird and will need reassurance constantly during the day and may need attention during the night to allay the night terrors common to this species. Cockatiels are also prone to nighttime panic; an awareness of this potential problem will allow you to prepare for this eventuality, and possibly prevent its occurrence.

Family Dinners

Some birds will not eat well unless they can do so in sight of their family. Flocks eat together, and birds are often more comfortable eating in a group with humans or other birds than alone.

One of my birds was particularly difficult to wean from baby formula to foods she could eat herself. She became almost impossible to feed, refusing the formula and anything else I offered her. One night, she sat on my TV tray as I began to eat some lemon pepper fish. Whether it looked good or smelled good, I will never know. She put her beak on the fish and tongued the inside of her beak for what seemed like a long time. I broke off a tiny piece and offered it to her. She rolled it around in her beak awhile and then swallowed and begged for more. I gave her a good portion, and was thrilled that she ate it. Today, this bird will not eat unless I am eating nearby. She eats what I eat. (You can only imagine the pressure this puts on me to plan healthful meals that my family and my bird will all enjoy.) I suspect that many hand-fed birds were weaned in similar fashion, eating with the breeder often enough that to the bird it becomes the norm.

Birds are usually comforted by eating together, or with their owners.

Noise, Blessed Noise

Noise is another factor in keeping your bird emotionally healthy. Wild birds use noise as a way to determine if all is well with their world. As an avidly interested observer of wild animals all over the world, I have taken particular delight in watching this phenomenon.

My grandson and I are often in the woods near my home. Squirrels jump from tree to tree, deer appear out of nowhere and crash through the forest when they see us, a roadrunner sometimes zips across our path and birds are everywhere singing to proclaim their territory. We can always tell when a predatory animal, such as a hawk, is near, though. The woods fall silent and animals that might be the hawk's prey sit motionless. When the hawk leaves, the forest sounds return to normal.

35

Pet birds retain this instinctive need for a certain amount of noise. In my home, we program the CD player to play all day, or we turn on the TV in the family room where the birds live. This seems to supply the amount of noise they need to preserve their sense of well-being.

Food as an Emotional Issue

A wild bird spends a good part of each day searching for food. The need for a steady, dependable food supply is a strong instinct in all birds. You know that you

will give your bird the food he needs each day, but he cannot read your mind. Set two feeding times a day, and stick to them steadfastly. Your pet will then come to expect his food at those times. If you are late or forget to feed your bird, you will cause your bird great stress, and stress can lead to illness. You can be late once in a while, but if you know you will not be able to feed your bird at a certain time, try to be early rather than late.

Your bird may also have an emotional response to the amount and kind of food you offer. Find out what kind of

Pet birds need noise around them and like to make noise as well.

food your bird is used to eating. Even if that is considered an inadequate diet for his species, offer enough of the familiar food with more healthful food so your bird does not panic. Birds don't adapt to change readily, especially changes in food. This is a survival technique, and a good one. Wild birds must know which foods they can eat and which foods are toxic. Presumably parents teach their chicks which foods to choose. Most birds will reject unfamiliar foods. If you continue to offer a food to your bird, and perhaps to eat some of the food in front of him on many occasions, he may try some, too.

When you put food in your bird's cage, be sure to offer enough that he will feel secure. Each bird is different, but you will get to know your bird's comfort level. Two of my birds need full seed cups and full bowls of fresh fruit and vegetables each day. Rosebud, my female

Eclectus, likes some seed, but not much, and a full bowl of fruits and vegetables. That's just a start for her, though. She also demands whatever we eat at each meal. Cooked food, for her, is a necessity. If we leave home for more than

part of a day, we hire someone to come in and feed her home-cooked food. The other two birds enjoy some cooked food, but are not as emotionally dependent on it as Rosebud.

When giving your bird new food, be patient; it may take some time before he'll try it.

Day Planner

Early on, decide how much time you can spend with your bird each day and plan that into your schedule.

When you first bring home your new pet, you will be enchanted, and will want to reassure him that he is all right. How better to do this than to pay as much attention to him as possible? You will probably train him to step onto your hand, to potty on cue, perhaps to talk. All this takes time—but it's time well spent.

Unfortunately, your regular duties, including your job, your family and normal everyday chores, will crowd back in on the charmed little life you have showered on your bird. You know you must get back to normal, but your pet has come to expect this level of interaction with

> **HOW TO IMPROVE YOUR BIRD'S EMOTIONAL HEALTH**
>
> - Pay lots of attention to him.
> - Praise, praise, praise him.
> - Place his cage where there is family activity.
> - Keep a radio or television on for comforting noise.
> - Schedule playtime for you and your bird.
> - Plan an interesting and varied diet.
> - Establish a routine and try to stick to it.

you. Soon, he may exhibit signs of frustration and unhappiness, such as screaming, refusal to eat, depression and feather plucking. You will be upset, perhaps convinced that you should never have brought a bird into your life.

MAKING TIME

There's a simple solution to this problem, though. Decide from the first how much time you can reasonably devote to your bird. Factor in your work schedule, whether you work at home or elsewhere, whether your bird can accompany you as you do some household chores and when the best time for interaction

Try your best to plan quality time with your bird every day.

with you occurs each day. If you like to read or watch television in the evenings, this might be a good time to play with your pet. He could sit on your knee or hand as you pet him and preen his head feathers.

If you work at home and have a relatively passive species, perhaps you can keep your bird with you all day, every day. I know of numerous people who do just that—and keep their birds' cages in their bedrooms, too.

For most of us, though, this is just not practical. I work at home, but could not get anything done if I let all of the birds out while I write. I know their personalities well, though, and use that knowledge to make workable choices.

BIRD PERSONALITIES

A Man's Bird—Doodle

Our Parrotlet is active in the morning. She prefers my husband to me and chews things constantly—anything in reach of her beak. She will readily destroy clothing and jewelry. In the morning, as we are preparing bird diets, Sherman puts an old towel around his shoulders and lets Doodle out of her cage. She chatters in his ear, chews the towel and snuggles the back of his neck while he walks around feeding animals and later, when he is at work in his home office.

The Destroyer—Gandalf

Gandalf, our Cockatoo, is destructive all the time and must be watched constantly. He stays in his cage until the afternoon, his most docile time of the day. Then he can come in my office and sit on the back of my chair as I work at my desk. Left to himself, he would chew the back of my chair, but we have covered that with an old, thick towel that he can chew at will.

The Complex Bird—Rosebud

Rosebud is the most complicated of our birds. A female Eclectus, she can be dangerously territorial. She relaxes in the evenings, though, just after she has eaten dinner with us. With a full crop, she will sit on my hand as I type or write, gazing into my face and making her charming little burble sounds. She and I spend most evenings together like this. In the daytime, though, she is content to stay in her cage, where she eats, rests and guards her food and toys. Periodically in the evening, I put her high above my head on my hand and encourage her to flap her wings until she is tired. She enjoys this form of exercise and so do I. When she is tired, I hug her and hold her close for a good five minutes.

If your new pet is a Finch, a Pekin Robin or a Canary, you might not have planned to take her out of her cage. You can train these birds to spend time out of the cage, as you would

ABOUT ROUTINES

My first learning experience about the importance of keeping a schedule was with my Cockatoo. When we brought him home, I worked out of the house every day, teaching school. I usually left home at 6 A.M. and did not return until about 6 P.M. The stereo was on all day, but other than our goldfish, Gandalf was home alone. In the evening, he came out to play. About three years after we had brought Gandalf home, our routine changed. We moved, and I stayed home for a year, gearing up for a career change. Sometimes, I let Gandalf out to spend the day with me, and sometimes I did not. On some days, I was home, but on others I was out all day. Gandalf began screaming and picking his feathers, classic signs of insecurity and unhappiness.

A year later, when I went back to work full time, Gandalf quit pulling his feathers. Routine, he was trying to say, is good. Any routine, just make it fairly constant. When my husband and I moved to our present home, the birds had to adjust to both of us staying home. This went off with few hitches, mainly because we developed a schedule and have stuck to it.

if you had a Parrot. Talk to a breeder, a vet or another person knowledgeable about the species to determine how much of your time this bird will need, especially compared to the amount of time you are willing to give. At the very least, a Canary or small Finch will need time when you are in the room with him, talking to him and feeding him tidbits. If you already have the bird and cannot give him the kind of attention he needs, perhaps you can get him a companion of the same species and opposite sex, or you can give him to someone who has time to devote to the bird. This will reduce your stress as well as your bird's.

Maintaining a regular cleaning and feeding schedule can help calm a small bird, such as a Canary, that might not be tame enough to come out of his cage. My Zebra Finches were not tame, but they accepted my care schedule in a more relaxed fashion when I did it at the same time each day.

So how much time each day can you reasonably expect to devote to your bird? Can you make those times relatively static? If so, both you and your bird will be happier.

One Bird or Two?

The temptation for first-time bird owners is to buy two birds. Many people believe that birds need a companion to be happy (especially in the case of the Lovebird—the name seems to imply that they need a partner). It's true that birds need companionship, but it need not be a bird. In fact, if you buy two birds, they will bond to each other and seek their needed affection from each other—even if they were hand-fed. They will tolerate you and may even interact with you, but the bond will not be as strong as it would have been had you bought only one bird.

On the other hand, if you buy only one bird, you will need to offer him the attention another bird would have given him. This doesn't mean twenty-four-hour-a-day tending: it means you will have to pay a reasonable amount of attention to the bird. He will need lots of playtime out of the cage and with you. You will find that he wants to cuddle and chirp at you—I can certainly think of less enjoyable activities.

It does take a lot of planning at first, though, to make playing with your bird a habit. If you cannot offer this kind of interaction, your bird may become emotionally damaged. Flock animals eat, sleep and play together. You will find that your bird will want to play with you and will eat best if you eat at the same time. He may even want to share your food with you. Not only is this a good "flock" activity, it is a good time to bond—and it is fun. So—one bird or two? The choice is yours and should be made before you make your purchase, depending on how much time you can devote to your bird and how close you want the relationship to be. If you are in doubt, buy one bird. If you find that you cannot give him enough attention, buy a second bird. You must find out before you purchase your birds if they will get along with each other. Certain birds, like Quaker parrots, are too aggressive to be housed with another bird. If you decide to buy two birds, choose another of the same species as your first bird. Mixing species could result in the death or injury of one of the birds.

Caring
for

part two

Your
Bird

chapter 4

Preparing
for Your
Bird

Before you actually buy a bird, find an avian vet. This may seem premature, but it will be one of the best things you can do to prepare for your new pet. Not all vets are avian vets; an avian vet must study birds and pass special exams to qualify for certification. The amount of information in this book on the special features of birds covers only a small part of what these specialists must know to become licensed.

Choosing an Avian Vet

To find an avian vet, you can call other vets in your area and ask for a referral. You can also attend a bird-club meeting and ask members for advice, or call *Bird Talk* magazine for a name and phone number; *Birds USA* magazine also has an avian-vet directory. You can also get in touch with a local wild-animal rehabilitation facility or bird rehabilitator for this information.

When you find an avian vet, make a prepurchase appointment. Ask for a tour of the vet clinic. It should be clean and the animals well cared for. The vet should be easy to talk to. Ask about the species of bird you intend to buy; potential health problems, feeding, caging and safety concerns are a few of the subjects you

can discuss. As you talk, decide whether you can communicate with this health professional.

Ask about emergency procedures. Does this vet handle them personally, or is there an emergency clinic in the area? Does that clinic have expertise in handling birds? Your

ability to communicate with your bird's vet will be vital during her lifetime. A warm, caring veterinarian can make all the difference in how long your bird will live and can make bonding with and caring for your new pet effortless.

Holistic avian veterinarians consider a bird's emotional, as well as physical, needs.

Expect to pay for a prepurchase visit to the vet. Veterinarians are professionals and their time is valuable. Before you make an appointment, call and get an estimate of how much the consultation will be. When you find an avian vet you like, make an appointment corresponding to the date and time you plan to buy your bird. On your way home from the store or breeder's facility, keep that appointment.

HOLISTIC AVIAN VETERINARIANS

Consider a holistic avian veterinarian. Holistic medicine for animals is a relatively new field, but it suits birds perfectly. This discipline takes the whole bird into consideration, including emotional and physical needs, to keep her healthy. You can find a holistic vet by logging on to this Web site: http://www.altvetmed. com. If you can find a holistic vet in your area, be sure to consider this important option.

READ UP

Before you bring home your bird, or shortly thereafter, read about her species and subspecies. Most small birds, including Finches, Canaries, Parrotlets and Pekin Robins, feel especially vulnerable in a world full of larger animals.

BUYING A CAGE

A proper cage is essential for your bird. Again, each species has special requirements. A good rule of thumb on cage size has long been "buy the largest you can afford." Take into account the width of cage bars; they should be too narrow for your bird to squeeze through and escape. Those tiny bones in your bird's body will help her squeeze through bars easily.

The cage bars should be narrow enough to prevent your bird from escaping.

In addition, some birds, especially small birds like Lovebirds, Finches, Canaries, Pekin Robins and Parrotlets, need cages taller than they are wide to allow them to fly from perch to perch. Perches should be placed on each end instead of having one or two perches placed lengthwise from end to end in the cage.

Keep it Simple

Before you buy a cage, make sure it is of a simple, easy-to-clean design. I've bought enough of those cages with curlicues on them to tell you they are a pain to clean. Now, I stick to simple designs, preferring those made of chrome, stainless steel or powder-coated metal.

Special Cages for Special Birds

Lorikeets pose a unique problem. These are beautiful, sociable birds, but they do have liquid droppings that they squirt on the walls and floors if you have not planned adequately. The best bet would be a large cage with the lengthwise perch in the center, and a wide apron around the outside to catch the bird's excrement.

Perhaps the best cage of all for a Lorikeet is a cage made of acrylic or glass. Sides are solid, with holes drilled for attaching perches, toys and food and water dishes. There are additional air holes on the top and sides as well. The sides should be easy to remove and clean. Before you buy such a cage, attempt to remove the side panels and then reassemble them.

Never place this bird's cage on carpet. If you are thinking about buying a Lorikeet, you must first commit yourself to taking your bird out of her cage regularly for long periods of time, and, yes, to cleaning up after her.

A Toucan needs a large cage that will accommodate her long bill and large body. However, Toucans are not destructive; their bills are not rigid enough to allow them to chew anything as hard as furniture, and their droppings are relatively easy to clean up. She should also have lots of time out of her cage.

Small birds, including Finches and Canaries, can be housed in bamboo or wooden cages, but you simply cannot put a Parrot, large or small, in such a cage. Even metal bars can be breached if they are of an appropriate size. My Cockatoo chewed through the bars of his first cage. A storm was raging outside, trees were falling over in our courtyard and the ocean was lapping at the lawn in front of the house. I was upstairs and he was frightened. It took him no time at all to chew his way out and climb upstairs to find me—even though we had not had him long and he was untamed. That taught me a lesson. That cage had bars of a size that was just fine for a Cockatiel, but was no barrier at all for a larger bird.

When you choose a cage for any bird, ask for help from knowledgeable pet-store personnel. If they are familiar with the species of the bird you have chosen, they can give you many tips about the cages they carry. If, for any reason, you don't see what you had in mind, keep shopping. It's best not to buy a used cage. It would be difficult to clean it well enough to remove all possible bacteria or viruses the cage might harbor from its former occupant.

PERCHES AND OTHER FURNITURE

Birds need a variety of sizes of perches to keep their feet healthy. This is important because birds sit on

Keep your bird's feet healthy by varying the sizes of her perches.

their feet all the time. A healthy bird will pull one foot up into her feathers to rest, but this is really the only relaxation for a bird's feet. Wild birds fly from tree limb to branch to the ground, and so on. This allows their feet to rest and exercise by exposing them to many types and sizes of perches.

We can do the same thing for our pets by providing a number of perches. I favor natural materials such as manzanita branches, which come in many sizes. The main perches should be large enough around that the bird's front and back toenails do not

quite meet when the bird is at rest. In addition, you can add the new cotton ropes and cement perches. For small birds, consider half perches that are only a few inches long. These will not disrupt your bird's flight path, but will give her a number of places to land. If you have a larger bird, such as a Macaw, a Cockatoo, an African Grey or a Lorikeet, you may still add one or two of these half perches for variety.

Choose perches in natural colors to help create comfortable surroundings for your bird. A few dowel-type perches are also adequate for Finches, Canaries, Pekin Robins, Parrotlets, Budgies and other small birds. Flat, wooden perches, in appropriate sizes, also help a bird rest her feet. Never put sandpaper-covered perches in a bird's cage. These can rub her feet raw, encouraging infection. These perches are touted as the perfect way to trim birds' toenails, but they don't do the job. You will need to learn to clip your bird's toenails anyway, and there is no reason to make her uncomfortable in an effort to make your life a little easier. (Clipping toenails is already easy.)

Some birds, such as Finches, will be happiest living in pairs. Supply them with a nest suitable to their species, as well as swings and plenty of perches to give them a variety of places to land as they flit about their cage.

CAGE-FLOOR COVERING

The covering of your bird's cage bottom is an important issue. Because your bird relieves herself about every fifteen minutes, drops excess food every time she eats and litters the cage bottom with endless other detritus, choosing a covering for this area will be a weighty decision.

The floor covering should be inexpensive, nontoxic and have a nice appearance. There are many brands and types on the market. A quick tour of pet stores will reveal those that cover the cage bottom in thick layers of absorbent material, such as ground corn cobs. The advantage is that the bird's droppings fall into this material and seem to disappear. The disadvantage is that you may be tempted to leave the corn cobs on the cage bottom for a long time. The material is expensive, and you might not want to throw it out frequently, much less daily. Worse, from my point of view, (and for your bird's health) is that any thick, ground medium will also harbor bacteria. Fungus will grow, and the unsanitary conditions will endanger your bird. By the time you can see the growths, if ever, your bird's health will be compromised.

I also discourage using sand. Never put beach sand on the bottom of your bird's cage; it can contain untold harmful bacteria. Sanitized sand for birds is available, but is especially messy and by its nature this medium encourages bacterial growth.

What's the best cage-bottom covering? I think the best is black-and-white newspaper. It is nontoxic, readily available and cheap. Because it costs just a few cents a day, you will be more likely to change it at least once a day. We take only the Sunday newspaper, and it is more than an ample supply for our birds' cages. If you have a small bird, you may want to use gravel-covered paper cut to fit the size of your bird's cage. For one cage, I use white paper towel.

WHERE SHOULD THE CAGE GO?

Your bird will be happiest in the center of family activity.

Finding just the right place for your bird's cage is an important task. If you put a lot of thought into it, you may never have to move the cage, which will give your bird security. You need to put your bird's home in a room where you and your family spend a lot of

time—such as a family room or an in-home office. Your bird will want to be at the center of family activity. Because birds are flock animals, they are most comfortable where you are.

Most birds will not want to be in the actual center of the action, however. They will prefer to be placed at the edge, against a wall or in a corner. This wall must be an inside wall to prevent vast changes in temperature. An outside wall, even one that backs on a garage, will become too cold in winter. No matter how well your home is insulated, an outside wall is unsuitable.

Locate all birds away from windows, which are a source of temperature fluctuations. Birds that can be seen from outside are also made more vulnerable to someone who might be looking for a valuable item to steal.

Depending on how strong your bird's fight-or-flight instincts are, she may be terrified by the sight of wild birds and other animals outside, which will cause her undue stress and may lead to illness.

Larger birds, such as large Parrots, Toucans, Touracos, Toucanets and Lorikeets, are more gregarious and less timid about the normal hustle and bustle of family life than are some smaller birds. Plan to locate these birds in the family room, or another area where you and your family spend most of your time. This way, your bird can take part passively in the family's activities when she is in her cage, and actively when you let her out. You can also place plants near a larger bird's cage, but she will chew and destroy any within her reach (including imitation plants), and she can reach quite a distance, even if she has her wings clipped.

Finally, the level of the top of the cage may be important. Some birds will become more aggressive, as if they feel superior to you, if they are able to sit higher than the level of your eyes. If you have purchased a cage that is taller than your eyes, keep your bird from sitting on top of the cage. Provide a perch or play gym where she can sit while out of her cage.

PLANTS FOR BIRDS

Small wild birds hide in vegetation from predators. It follows, then, that small pet birds will feel most comfortable if they are provided with some kind of hiding place. A cage is wide open from any angle. You can make it more bird-friendly, though, by adding either real or imitation plants around the outside of the cage, on

---

SAFE PLANTS

bromeliads

scheffleras

African violets

miniature roses

ferns

begonias

Thanksgiving and
Easter cactuses

hibiscus

Mango trees

Dracaena

any type of ficus trees

bottle palms

ponytail palms

Unless you plan to replace plants regularly, place plants out of reach of your bird. Over time, imitation plants will probably be less expensive, unless you have a green thumb and are observant enough to watch out for the state of your plants' health.

three sides. You can also add to a small bird's sense of security by placing her cage next to an inside wall; an outside wall, one that faces the outside of the house—or even the garage—will be too cold in winter.

If you surround a bird's cage with plants, choose only those known to be nontoxic and nonirritating. Please see the sidebar on the previous page for some examples of safe plants.

TOYS

Toys are a necessary addition to any cage, and should be based strictly on your bird's species and size. A toy that's too large for a small bird, such as a Finch, might entrap a toenail or toe. Too many small birds break their delicate bones trying to extricate themselves from large toys they've become caught in. A small bird that catches a toenail in a toy will try to pull her leg free. If she breaks her toenail above the blood vessel line, she may bleed to death unless you notice her and take appropriate action soon enough to save her.

Small toys may injure large birds, too. Large birds have strong jaws. If given an opportunity to chew on small toys, they can easily break them, perhaps swallowing a jagged piece or cutting themselves on pieces sitting around their cages.

Appropriate toys are not only fun for your bird, they are necessary. Birds have active minds, well suited to hunting for food and water, hiding from predators and protecting their chicks. When we cage them, we need to provide enough diversion to keep their minds occupied. Small birds might enjoy toys that offer pieces of nesting material or mirrors. Larger birds are more likely to want toys they can destroy. Wooden toys meet those needs perfectly. Don't try to make them yourself, though, unless you can find wood that is not pressure

Toys should be checked regularly for loose pieces and sharp edges.

Caring for Your Bird

52

treated. Such treated woods are often found at home-improvement stores. The chemicals used repel or kill insects, and may be toxic to birds.

Companies that make wooden bird toys use untreated wood and specially made leather without tannins, safe for birds to chew, swallow and destroy. Even craft leather is not safe for birds. Some of the bird-toy companies treat their own leather to be sure it is safe. Increasingly, you can buy wonderful bird toys at pet and bird specialty stores. There are many remarkable toys available, too, from small companies that sell by direct mail only. You can find their advertisements in bird-related magazines.

If you buy colored toys, consider purchasing those in the same color range as your bird's feathers or those of a bird of the opposite sex. This will make her feel more comfortable. I first heard this theory from a long-time bird-toy maker several years ago. It made sense to me, so I bought a number of toys to match my various birds. I have to say, my birds prefer those toys that

Toys will stimu-late your bird's mental health and give her lots of entertainment.

match them. Choose only toys that have been dyed with food coloring or food-based colors or natural dyes considered safe for consumption.

My Cockatoo favors his toys that are yellow and white. Rosebud cuddles in her purple tent and mouths her red and purple beads first and foremost. The most striking example, though, is our Parrotlet, Doodle. While her mate, Yankee, was alive, the two fought constantly, but then made up and cuddled. They ate together, bathed together and slept next to each other like cute little salt and pepper shakers. When Yankee died,

we were seriously concerned. What would she do without her constant companion? We attached a green, blue and yellow cloth and leather toy to the top of her cage. It fluffs out into a kind of a tent, which she sleeps under. When she is angry at us, she attacks the toy. It has, as much as can be expected, taken the place of Yankee. She is very comfortable with that toy, perhaps more so than she was with her mate—it doesn't fight back.

Place a few toys in your bird's cage before you put her in it for the first time. She should have enough to entertain her, but not enough to crowd her. If she is a Canary, Parrotlet, Finch or Lovebird, place the toys away from the bird's flight path in the cage; do not place toys in between parallel perches on each end of the cage.

Keep extra toys on hand to replace any that become soiled. You should replace toys every week or so—with the exception of favorite toys. This will help occupy your bird's mind, ensuring mental health. Clean them in the dishwasher and put them away to rotate in again later.

FOOD AND WATER DISHES

You can never have too many food and water dishes. You will need at least one set per day, and probably two, with an extra set to replace the used dishes.

In general, I prefer stainless-steel or ceramic dishes, especially for larger birds. If any of your plastic or ceramic dishes develop chips or cracks, discard them right away. Bacteria can lurk in those crevices.

Water tubes are great for supplying water to your birds. These are made of glass or plastic and are attached to the side of a bird's cage. The spout is usually made of stainless steel. A ball at the tip of the spout is often red, which seems to tempt the bird to touch it with her tongue; that's when she learns that it contains water. Keep several of these on hand, too, because you will need to replace and clean them daily.

If you are introducing a bird to a water tube, also offer her water in a regular dish until you are sure she has learned to get her water from the tube. Watch her droppings to be sure that she is not dehydrated from a lack of water. For smaller birds or those birds that require nectar (such as Lorikeets), feeding tubes are made for seeds and for nectar. Check into both, but remember that they need to be changed frequently. Sugar is a good medium for bacterial growth.

Large Parrots enjoy dumping food dishes. For this reason, I like stainless-steel dishes that screw to the outside of the cage—with attachments far from the curious beaks of my pets. If you choose this arrangement, it will save you a lot of cleaning chores. To keep up with the latest innovations in any cage accessories, take regular tours of pet stores and read the advertisements in bird-related magazines. You will be pleasantly surprised; most are safe, innovative, reasonably priced and attractive. The final responsibility for the safety and practicality of any choice, though, is yours.

Keep 'Em Clean!

Washing the bird's food and water dishes in the dishwasher is the best way to sanitize them. The strong detergent used and the hot drying temperatures in a dishwasher kill bacteria and viruses. When you wash these dishes by hand, the water might not be hot enough to kill these threats to your bird's health. Also, drying dishes with cloth dishtowels is a known way to spread bacteria. To be absolutely safe, you would have to hand wash these dishes separately from your own and any other bird's (and other pets as well) in scalding hot water and lots of detergent. To dry them, you would need to use paper towels, which would not harbor the bacteria that hides in cloth. It's simpler, however, to put these dishes in the dishwasher.

Bringing Birdie Home
TRAVEL CAGES

When you pick up your bird, take a travel cage with you. If the bird is tiny, such as a Parrotlet or a Finch,

consider a small, box-like cage with air holes in its top. The plastic carriers manufactured for hamsters and gerbils work well if you secure the top to the bottom with an elastic band around the whole cage. Line the cage with white paper towels. If your trip is short, add only a sprig of millet. If you will drive or fly for more than about thirty minutes, add a small cup of fruits and vegetables for moisture. Water will spill in the travel case, making your bird uncomfortable.

If you have chosen a larger bird and will travel by car, you have several options. At least

A plastic travel cage will help protect your bird from drafts.

one travel cage on the market folds to suitcase proportions, but comes in a variety of sizes that can accommodate small-to-large-size birds, such as Quaker Parrots, Cockatiels, African Greys and Macaws. Its perches sit low in the cage, so the bird will not have far to fall if she loses her balance. Removable, washable dishes come with the cage and fit into its sides.

Other travel cages made for birds are made of acrylic. These cages generally do not fold into smaller shapes for storage, but are sturdy and prevent drafts from stressing your bird. These can be custom made with smoked acrylic to give your bird a greater sense of security. You can order acrylic cages for small-to-large birds.

If you will travel by plane to reach your home, call the airline at least a month in advance—further beforehand for holiday travel—to reserve a space in the passenger cabin for your bird. Only one pet can travel in each section of the plane. If you fail to call early enough, your bird will need to travel in the pet section of the baggage compartment in the bottom of the plane. In any case, travel by plane will require a great deal of thought about preventing the bird's escape from the travel cage, food placement and avoiding drafts. I would use only a plastic travel cage because a cage with bars gives a bird less protection from temperature changes that occur on a plane.

Take weather into consideration when you plan your trip home with your bird. If the weather is hot, place your bird's travel cage away from the air-conditioning vent in your car. Sudden changes in temperature will add further stress to a bird that is already anxious about what is happening. Stress can reduce the effectiveness of the bird's immune system, making her more susceptible to disease. For the same reason, place the bird's travel cage out of direct sunlight, which will quickly overheat your bird.

In the winter, wrap a blanket around the travel cage to carry the bird from the store or breeder's facility to your car. If you can, preheat the car before you put your bird in it, but do not overheat it; this will cause the temperature change from the car to your home to be too dramatic.

> ## PUTTING YOUR BIRD IN HER CAGE
>
> There are several important guidelines to keep in mind when you move your bird from her travel cage to her main cage. Before you make this attempt, put food and water in the cage. Make sure toys are well placed, and turn on some calming music.
>
> - Never use gloves. Birds are afraid of hands and if you wear gloves, you simply compound the problem. If your bird becomes frightened, she may bite, but she is less likely to bite if you can calm her. To do this effectively, you must remain unruffled yourself.
>
> - Move slowly and talk softly to your bird in a lilting tone. It doesn't matter what you say; just use reassuring tones and mannerisms.
>
> - Have as few people in the room as possible. If you can, transfer your bird with no children around. Make sure there are no other pets in the room.

A TRIP TO THE VET'S OFFICE

On your way home with the bird, stop at the office of your avian veterinarian. Ask your vet to give your bird a thorough check-up, for both mental and physical well-being. This may involve taking some blood and fecal samples for cultures to determine if your bird has been infected with any bacterial or viral disease. This costs more than an external exam, but is necessary to determine the bird's state of health. While you are in the veterinarian's office, ask him or her to trim your bird's toenails and show you how to do it. Also ask the vet to clip your bird's wings. Observe carefully so you can do it yourself in the future.

Introducing Your New Bird to the Cage

When you walk into your home, remember that although this is familiar ground to you, your bird

Give your new bird several days to adjust to her cage and the activity around her.

has never seen it before. Instinctively, a bird, even one that was hand-fed, will be stressed by the number of changes she has had to endure on this one day in her life.

She will be frightened and unsure of what may happen next. Place the travel cage near the bird's cage, in full view. (If you have other birds, quarantine the new bird without fail. See the section on quarantine later in this chapter.)

Keep the situation as calm as possible. If you have other pets, secure them in another part of the house or outside. Young children should stay away for a few hours. Playing soothing music in the background will give assurance to the bird that all is well.

Sit near the travel cage. You can read or watch television, but avoid direct eye contact with the bird for the first half hour or so, giving her time to look at her surroundings. After that period of time, or when the bird begins to move around a bit in her travel cage, put the open door of the travel cage next to the open door of the cage, letting the bird come out on her own to get into her cage.

If your bird fails to come out on her own, or if the cage doors do not fit well, open the door of the travel cage to allow the bird to perch there. When she does, put a perch under her abdomen and push up gently, putting the bird slightly off balance. (You can actually see this process, so you will know how far to take it. Simply move slowly.) This will force her to step up on the perch. Slowly move the bird into her cage, allowing her to step onto a perch in the cage.

Allow your bird to remain in her cage for the rest of the day and for several more days so that she can gain confidence that you mean her no harm. From the point at which you buy your bird, through the rest of her life, your job is to earn and maintain your bird's trust.

Although you may reduce the activity in your home for the first few hours after you bring your bird home, return it to normal as soon as possible. Your bird will feel more comfortable with noise in the house and she will eventually have to get used to your and your family's regular activity.

QUARANTINE

If you already have any other birds, place the new bird in quarantine for at least a month—preferably eight weeks. Discuss this with your avian vet. At the beginning of the quarantine period, ask your vet to take a fecal sample to culture for any likely disease. Do not let your bird come in contact with your other birds until she has a clean bill of health from your avian vet.

Quarantine involves separating your bird from any others by placing her in her own room. When you feed your new bird, always keep her dishes separate from those of your older bird(s). Wash your hands thoroughly with hot water and soap, and dry them on paper towels to reduce the chance of spreading disease from your new bird to older birds. Wash all bird-care utensils, including dishes and toys, in the dishwasher, where the caustic soap and hot drying cycle will help sterilize them.

Any time you handle your new bird or clean her cage, wash and dry your hands. If you suspect that your new bird has an illness that could put your old bird(s) in danger, change clothes, shower and wash your hair between handling new and old birds. Diseases can be carried between birds on your body hair, as well as on your clothes. Quarantine is serious business.

IMPORTANT OBSERVATIONS

During the days you let your bird rest and become accustomed to you and her new surroundings, take the time to observe her discreetly but thoroughly. This is

the perfect time to notice what your bird's eyes look like, and how her feathers lie on her body. Watch to see how she grooms herself and how long she takes to complete this job.

Take a look at her droppings once a day when you change the cage paper. If you've fed her something red, such as strawberries, notice the difference in the appearance of her droppings several hours later.

Getting Baseline Information

Keep track of how much your bird eats and when. Note which perches she prefers to sit on when resting,

Get to know your bird's routine, including how much she eats and when she is most active.

playing and eating. Learn about her bathing habits. All of this bird-watching is for a purpose. This is the base-line information against which you can compare her appearance and actions to determine if she is unwell. Variation from the norm necessitates a trip to your avian vet. The earlier you notice a variation, the better your chance of helping your bird regain her health.

Remember, birds hide any sign of illness as long as they can; predators attack sick birds for an easy kill. The choice between a slow, sick bird and a fast, healthy bird is easy for a predator to make. The bird's only defense is to pretend she is well as long as she can. Usually, by the time a bird is obviously ill, such as sitting on the bottom of her cage, she is near death. Observing your new bird's routine in the beginning will help you monitor her health throughout her lifetime.

chapter 5

Your
Bird's
Nutrition

Years ago, the best advice bird owners were able to gather indicated that birds ate only seeds. Unfortunately, too many people today still believe this is true. This would translate, roughly, to humans restricting their diets to bread and water.

A Varied Diet = Good Health

A seed-only diet for most birds is severely deficient in nutrients necessary to maintain life. For this reason, the average life span of pet birds in North America is approximately 5 years—even for larger birds that should have life expectancies of at least 50 years. Learning that one fact was jolting to me. By restricting our birds to unhealthful diets, we are, in effect, starving them to death.

Over the years, my birds have shown me that they want more than seeds, and I have let their tastes be my guide. Encouraged by their interest in the food the human members of my family eat, I offered them food considered healthful. I also began to pay close attention to the diets of wild birds and to talk to avian vets on the subject.

Fortunately for those of us who love our birds— and most of all for the birds themselves—we know a lot about what to feed birds. This body of knowledge continues to grow, however, and requires constant reappraisal. To date, the best studied bird diets are those of Cockatiels and Finches, including Canaries.

Birds that are fed a healthful diet can live at least 50 years.

WHAT DO BIRDS EAT IN THE WILD?

The most obvious way to answer the question of what each species needs to support optimum health would seem to be to study what each species eats in the wild. Aviculturists have attempted this for some time, but with mixed results. A species must rely on what it can find during times of drought as well as normal rainfall. To determine all of the foods a species needs to reach peak health would involve many years of arduous work, following several flocks in various locations and then analyzing the data. To date this has proven a formidable goal.

As with human nutrition, we now believe that a variety of healthful foods is the key to good health in birds. Birds of all species need a certain amount of fat, protein, minerals and vitamins in their diets, but each species requires different foods. As the species has developed, those members that ate certain foods thrived and reproduced. In captivity, we can occasionally approximate the nutritional needs of a species, but sometimes we fail miserably.

Caring for
Your Bird

This chapter on nutrition can act as a guide, especially as a means to alert you to the importance of nutrition. However, because each species has special needs, check with your veterinarian on exactly what foods and proportions of foods and other nutrients your bird needs to thrive.

A varied diet comprised of nutritious foods is optimal for your bird's well-being.

Fresh Seeds

While seeds should not make up a bird's whole diet, they form a good base. It's critical to use fresh seed because it contains the most nutrients. You can easily find out if seed is fresh by trying to sprout it. Cut a piece of a new sponge. Put it in a small bowl of water until it has absorbed the water. Place the wet sponge on a small plate in the sun and sprinkle some seeds on the top, working them into the holes of the sponge. Keep the sponge damp and fresh seeds will sprout. Do not feed these to your bird because you have not controlled the possible growth of bacteria or mold.

KEEPING SEEDS FRESH

Keeping seeds fresh is easy, especially if you buy them in fairly small lots. The actual amount you buy will depend largely on the number of birds you own. As soon as you get home with the seeds, put them in the freezer. Leave them there for at least twenty-four hours to kill all the seed moths or other insects that may have infested the bag or box. If you have a sealable container, you can store them in that. To do so, take the bag or box of seeds from the freezer, and let them reach room temperature before you open the parcel in which they were purchased. Then pour them into the jar. Replace the lid and adjust it so it's tight enough to prevent an infestation of insects.

The Role of Grit in a Bird's Diet

The only pet birds that require the addition of grit to their diets are Doves and Pigeons. These birds do not hull seeds they eat and need grit to help break down and digest their food.

Pelleted Food for Birds

Pellets for pet birds were developed and first marketed in the early '80s. They were highly controversial then and, to some degree, remain so today.

The main problem with many pelleted foods in the '80s was that they were introduced as a complete diet: convenient, easy to use and best for every bird. They were definitely easy to use and convenient. It looked like the way to end all that fruit and vegetable mess and the problem with offering a healthful variety of foods.

The first dilemma many pet owners noticed was acceptance. Pellets did not look like any food our pet birds had eaten before; birds resist anything unfamiliar, and some starved to death rather than eat that odd-looking stuff.

Another problem was boredom. Can you imagine eating the same thing every day—no matter how good it is for you? That alone could cause enough stress to impair a bird's immune system, which would leave it wide open to a number of serious diseases. Perhaps the major problem was that little research had gone into the first pelleted food.

SPROUTING SEEDS

Sprouted seeds are a valuable addition to any bird's diet. Sprouting them is easy, but must be done carefully. The best candidates are millet, wheat, oat and sunflower seeds.

For one or two birds, place a tablespoonful of seeds in a bowl. Cover them with tepid water. Cover the bowl and leave it for about twelve hours in a warm area, or twenty-four hours in a cold area. Rinse the seeds well, looking carefully for any that ooze a liquid or look as if they may have fungi or mold growing on them.

If many in the batch are spoiled, throw them all out. Dry the good seeds on a paper towel and feed them to your birds. Throw away any they do not eat in about four hours to avoid the possibility of digestive upsets due to spoiled food.

Without exhaustive research, it was impossible to produce a food that was truly complete for any species. Dr. Tom Roudybush at the University of California at Davis made a great breakthrough when he studied Cocka-tiels thoroughly and developed the first truly complete pelleted food for a bird species. Today, there are several pelleted foods on the market that were developed by avian vets. These come closest to meeting a bird's nutritional needs, and when you choose a brand, one developed by an avian veterinarian should be at the top of your list.

Should you offer your bird only pellets? Opinions differ, but I think that a diet of only pellets is a poor choice. No matter how complete a pelleted diet may be, it can become boring. We already fight boredom in caged birds. These are animals that have developed for thousands of years. The basis of survival for those that have been successful is the ability to seek food. Birds spend a great portion of each day hunting for sustenance. This quest keeps their minds active, their bodies fit. By making birds into pets, we remove this need to hunt for food, but that gives them a great deal of leisure time. That time must be filled with some other activity. We supply toys to fill part of their time, some hours are taken up with playing with us and sleeping, but the rest of each day is devoted to eating. If they have seeds, fresh fruits and vegetables and cooked food in addition to pellets, they can eat a balanced diet that is also interesting.

Food Preparation
FRESH FRUITS AND VEGETABLES

An important part of nutrition and the health of your bird is preparing his food. Before you shop for fresh fruits and veggies each week, clean your refrigerator's crisper drawers with warm water and soap. Rinse with hot water and dry with paper towels. Cloth towels may harbor bacteria dangerous to your birds. Line these drawers with white paper towels.

Freshness Is Important
Buy the freshest vegetables. If possible, buy those fresh foods certified free of any pesticides or herbicides. Buying only organic foods does not necessarily ensure

that they are free of pesticides. There are those who claim a product was grown organically when it was not. Be aware, too, that even authentically organic produce may be packed in the same facility that handles non-organic food, resulting in exposure to nonhygienic sur-

faces. In other words, wash all fresh fruit and vegetables carefully. There are several ways to do this. You can wash them with copious amounts of running water, or you can wash them in a mild detergent and water solution, and then rinse them prudently, removing all traces of soap, which could make your bird sick.

Cleaning the Produce

If you are especially concerned about the cleanliness of the produce available in your area, you can buy Nolvasan, a disinfectant nontoxic to birds, from your avian veterinarian. Soak fresh fruits and vegetables in a solution of Nolvasan and water. Rinse and dry, as usual. Spread white paper towels on your kitchen counters. Put the washed fruits and vegetables there to air dry before you place them in the crisper drawers. To make it easy if you have several bird species, use one drawer for fruit and one for vegetables. This will simplify food preparation. Before you work with fresh food in your kitchen, make sure all surfaces are clean and, especially, free of any liquid that might have seeped from meat or poultry products. If you use a cutting board, wash it in the dishwasher between uses. I even put my wooden cutting boards in the dishwasher. Use only utensils and dishes that have been sterilized in the dishwasher.

Preparing and cleaning your bird's food is an important part of keeping her healthy.

Remove fresh fruits and vegetables from your bird's cage long before they spoil. The amount of time will vary, depending on the temperature in your home. Of course, you will be vigilant in the summer because of the warm temperatures, but also be cautious in the winter, when you heat your home enough to spoil food in just a few hours.

Fresh food should be promptly removed from your bird's cage after he eats it.

COOKED FOODS

Cooked foods offer an excellent source of nutrition to many bird species. The easiest way to offer healthful food to your bird is to feed him what you eat—provided you eat nutritious food. If you subsist on junk food, cook special food for your bird.

To do this, you can cook medium-to-large quantities of food and freeze them in plastic freezer bags. Just before you feed your bird, microwave one bag of food, stir well to remove any hot spots created by the microwave-cooking method, let cool until it is warm and then serve. My birds will not eat the same thing day after day—and why should they? Make several meals and freeze them to alternate.

Not Too Hot!

The introduction of the microwave changed the way many of us cook, especially the way we reheat food. The convenience comes with some dangers, though, especially for birds. When you heat food in a microwave, hot spots develop and the food cooks unevenly. For humans, it doesn't pose a great problem, but for birds, the danger can be fatal. A young bird tends to gulp food in hunks as big as he can get into his mouth. The food then quickly goes into the bird's crop, which is made of thin, delicate skin. If the food is too hot or has a spot that is too hot, the skin will burn, perhaps becoming a scorched hole. If you don't discover the problem in time and then find a veterinarian able to repair the wound surgically, the bird will die.

The solution is simple; stir any food you cook in the microwave until you have equalized the temperature in all parts. This is especially important in foods like cooked cereals and rice or those with dairy products, such as cheese, that can be swallowed quickly. If in doubt, use a food thermometer to check various parts of the food. If the food placed on the inside of your wrist is too hot, it's too hot for your bird.

Most birds learn not to gulp food as soon as they are out of the chick stage. The gulping is a reflex to help a chick swallow food quickly when it's offered. This is a survival instinct. Those chicks that cannot beg loudly enough or grab and swallow proffered food quickly enough will not survive. The same instincts are found in hand-reared chicks.

Young birds tend to gulp their food, so be sure that their food is properly cooled to prevent burns.

Because we can anticipate this behavior and we know that microwaves heat food unevenly, we can prevent this injury. Even though all of my birds are past the chick stage, I still cool their food before I give it to them. They trust me to treat them with care; how can I do less?

Feeding Canaries and Finches

Canaries derive most nutritional elements necessary for their good health from a good Canary seed mix comprised of millet, Canary seed, hemp, maw, rape and niger. Offer small Finches a mix that contains mostly yellow or pancium millet; larger Finches require a larger proportion of white proso millet in their seed mix. Songbirds, such as Goldfinches, need song-food mixture comprised of dark, oily seeds such as niger, flax, hemp and rape. Read packages carefully to make sure the ingredients match your bird's needs.

Although a product may be labeled for Finches or Canaries, it does not necessarily contain all the required ingredients.

Also include vegetables in their diets each day. These should include leafy, dark-green lettuces, such as romaine, as well as kale and spinach. Birds need greens to help supply the phosphorous necessary for bone growth. Organically grown dandelion can also be offered. Note, however, that some produce labeled "organic" has nonetheless been treated with pesticides. If in doubt, it is not difficult to grow your own.

Small birds also enjoy fruit. If they've never seen it before, it may take a while to gain their confidence. Offer it daily, a slice of apple, pear or orange, for instance, until they recognize it as something that will not harm them. At that point, they may try it. Once a fruit is accepted, continue to offer it, but add one other type, until they have accepted several. Later, you can alternate them. Whatever you offer, though, must not have a hard surface that they cannot break through. Offer a slice of apple, not the whole apple. Remove all seeds from fruit, especially apple seeds.

Canaries need a good seed mix along with vegetables and fruit in their diet.

Do not pick wild greens for your birds; they may have been sprayed with insecticides or herbicides. In addition to seeds, fruit and greens, give these small birds a calcium source to peck at. Traditionally, bird keepers offered their birds cuttlebone, the skeleton of the Cuttlefish. In the last fifteen years or so, Cuttlefish have lived in increasingly polluted waters, and we have reason to believe enough of the pollutants are stored in the bone to harm our birds. Instead, offer a good-quality mineral block for your bird to peck at.

Feeding Waxbills

Waxbills need live food to maintain optimum health. You can feed them small mealworms (larger mealworms have tough skin that will be difficult for a Waxbill to penetrate), white worms, aphids, fruit flies or wax worms. Many of these live food sources are easy to grow yourself. Mealworms, for instance, can be grown in an old aquarium. Place three layers of burlap in an aquarium, and add bran under each piece of cloth. Put a piece of apple in each layer. Add a few mealworms. They will propagate readily. Spray with enough water to keep the burlap damp, but not so much that you grow mildew or fungi. You can check often for progress. Fruit flies are just as easily propagated in a jar with a piece of cut banana for food.

Feeding Parrots

Wild Parrots eat many foods, including seeds, fruits, vegetables and meat. We should use this information to guide us in how to feed our pet birds. Very few foods that we eat are off limits to Parrots. If it is healthful for you to eat, it is more than likely beneficial for your bird, too. Avoid offering avocados, chocolate, alcohol, salty foods, sugary foods, fatty foods such as fried food, apple seeds and fruit pits, which can contain toxins. Never offer a bird rhubarb leaves; they are poisonous to birds as well as to humans.

Parrots can eat most foods that are healthful for you, but not avocados, chocolate, alcohol or junk food.

Offer such foods as eggs and cheese in moderation. Birds love them, but they're high in fat. Do offer lean meat and cooked chicken bones: Larger birds enjoy cracking them open for the marrow.

If you really get into nutrition, your own diet will improve as you begin to plan around your bird. We eat a lot of salads, both fruit and green; broiled meats, especially chicken and fish; whole wheat bread; pasta-based dishes and brown rice. These are as good for your birds as they are for you.

Small Parrots, such as Budgies and Parrotlets, eat many of the same foods as larger Parrots, but their beaks are not as strong. Remember to grate carrots and cut open such foods as tomatilloes, jalapeño peppers and nuts. These little Parrots also enjoy broccoli, carrot and beet tops; chickweed; dandelions; cooked corn and peas. Also offer small bits of cooked tofu or egg.

Feeding Toucans and Touracos

These birds are often referred to in literature as soft-bills, although there is nothing soft about their bills. These beautiful animals make good pets and have suffered the consequences of poor diets far too long.

Feed Toucans and Touracos fruit—fresh fruit. Each day offer them a mix of fruit cut into pieces. Avoid any citrus fruit, including lemons, oranges, tangerines, grapefruit and tangelos, as well as pineapples and tomatoes. Acid fruits interfere with the metabolism of these birds.

Many Touracos and Toucans have died from a condition known as iron-storage disease. This is thought to be caused by citric acid (in citrus fruits and all other acid fruits), which can cause excess iron to be stored in the bird's liver. Rely on a diet of whole grapes, diced apples, papaya, bananas, cooked fresh beets and carrots, supplemented by pelleted food made for your bird's species. If you are unsure about offering a food type to these birds, call a zoo near you that has Toucans or Touracos. The curator can offer you advice about food available in your area.

QUICK AND HEALTHY MEALS

Some foods your bird will enjoy that are easy to make at the last minute include oatmeal, quinoa, scrambled or boiled eggs, broiled or baked poultry, baked yams, lean baked or broiled beef and baked plantains.

Beans are a good source of nutrition for many birds. If you mix two or three types of beans (avoid dried lima beans), such as kidney and pinto with split peas and brown rice, you have made a tasty, nutritious dish for your bird.

A good rule of thumb for recipes you share with your bird: Keep fat, salt and sugar levels low.

Pasta is another favorite of birds, and the colorful vegetable pastas are a particular hit with most birds.

Feeding Lories and Lorikeets

Lories and Lorikeets have special food requirements. This need not scare you away from these lovely birds; if you are well informed, you can feed them properly. Wild Lories and Lorikeets eat fruit, pollen, nectar and small seeds. Their droppings are liquid, which they expel with force.

Captive Lorikeets and Lories should eat basically the same diet as wild birds. Offer them nectar (available commercially), diced fresh fruit, leafy green vegetables, shredded carrots, whole-grain bread, seeds and a dry Lory/Lorikeet diet. Although some "experts" may suggest to you that a dry diet alone is sufficient, such a diet will lead to the early death of your bird. The reason some people advise this diet is that it reduces the liquidity of the bird's droppings. Healthy Lories and Lorikeets have liquid droppings. To accommodate that, house them properly in an acrylic cage, or one that is solid on three sides, to prevent the droppings from spraying on the surrounding floor. If you cannot tolerate the liquid droppings, choose another bird.

> **KEEPING TRACK**
>
> Your record of what your bird eats will help you in another dramatically important way. Poor appetite may be the first sign of illness. If you know with certainty what and how much your bird eats each day, you will notice immediately when something is wrong, before it gets to a critical stage.

chapter 6

Grooming
Your
Bird

Wild birds spend a great deal of time grooming. This includes bathing and preening their own feathers and those of their flock mates. Some birds bathe in dust or dirt; most bathe in water. All pet birds should bathe in water. For a bird, grooming is not a matter of looking good; it's a matter of life or death.

Poorly groomed feathers will not support flight. Without the ability to fly, a normally airborne wild bird will die. She cannot find food; she cannot escape predators or complete any other normal function of her life. Unkempt feathers will not repel water, which will also make it impossible to fly. Soaked feathers will allow the bird to become chilled, stressing the bird's system and making her susceptible to disease. A bird that looks disheveled will attract the attention of predators looking for unhealthy prey—far easier to catch than a healthy bird.

The Grooming Instinct

The grooming instinct is strong in all birds. As birds developed over thousands of years, only those that had this instinct survived long enough to breed and pass along their genes. Grooming a bird is easy, especially compared to the efforts dog and cat owners must exert— or even the effort it takes you to prepare for each day.

BATHING

Offer your bird a chance to bathe every day. This can be accomplished in several ways. Pet stores sell baths that attach to the side of a bird cage. If you own a kind of bird that will get in this bath or is small enough to get in, it's a good way to offer a bath because it keeps the mess under control. Most small-to-medium-size birds, such as Finches, Canaries, Parrotlets, Cockatiels and Quaker Parrots, will take a bath in a shallow dish. Make sure the water just covers your bird's feet and that she can easily get out of the bath dish. Birds cannot swim and may have difficulty flying with wet feathers.

A shallow bath dish is all you need for a small bird.

Most larger birds, and some small and medium birds as well, enjoy bathing in the mist of a spray bottle. Always use fresh, warm water to spray your bird. Establish a routine and use the same spray bottle every time; use that bottle for nothing else to reduce the risk of exposing your bird to a dangerous chemical. Using an indelible marker, mark the side of the bottle with your bird's name.

75

There are bird bath products on the market to add to bathing water for birds, but they are not necessary. Water is far superior to any product you can buy. People who show birds know the benefits of a water bath; before a judge sees a bird her owner will spray her with water or provide water in a dish for her to bathe on her own.

The Importance of Bathing

Recently, aviculturists have noticed that pet birds that cannot bathe regularly or as often as they wish may begin picking their feathers. The feather picking continues even after these same birds have the opportunity to bathe regularly.

We knew there was probably a connection, but were unclear what that might be. After studying species that may begin picking feathers for this reason, some have developed a theory. Many otherwise emotionally and physically healthy birds that pull feathers for lack of bathing come from humid jungle climates. Their species developed in areas where rain falls daily—perhaps several times each day. Tropical birds bathe in rain, and as these species evolved over time, those birds that adapted best to such conditions thrived.

After bathing, most birds will preen their feathers until they shine.

We have taken these birds, such as Eclectus Parrots, out of their tropical environment and brought them into our dry homes, which are often in dry climates, as well. These birds often begin to pull their feathers when they are quite young and then will not quit. It's such a shame to see these lovely birds with picked feathers and to listen to their owners' anguished stories.

Wet feathers cause a bird to preen aggressively, putting every feather in place. As she preens, she will rub her head in the feathers at the base of her tail, where many birds have an oil gland. This oil spreads out on the feathers through her preening, making her feathers glisten. If she is a Cockatoo, Cockatiel or African Grey, she will rub her head in the areas where the feathers break down into powder, covering her feathers with it.

Trimming Nails

Grooming also involves trimming toenails. Before you do it for the first time, ask your avian veterinarian to do it and to show you how. If your bird has light-colored toenails, you can see the blood vein in each. Before you begin the trimming session, assemble the tools. It's best to do this out of your bird's sight. She will soon begin to know the signs and might panic when she sees the implements.

NAIL-TRIMMING TOOLS

To clip nails, you will need cornstarch, flour or styptic powder to staunch any blood flow if you cut the nails too far back. I prefer cornstarch. It works well and does not sting the bird. My birds have all reacted in pain when we have used styptic powder.

You will also need clippers or scissors made for the purpose. I prefer fingernail clippers. Again, I use one clipper for each bird and do not interchange. Family members are not

> **BATHING BIRD-STYLE**
>
> All of my three Parrots belong to species that came from humid jungles. All demand frequent baths. It's such a simple solution to a heartbreaking problem. When Rosebud, my Eclectus, wants a bath, she runs to the sink and stretches her wings out to catch the water. If I have a towel on the counter she waddles over and begins to pantomime the bath. Even if I am busy, I stop what I'm doing to fill her spray bottle, lay clean towels on the counter and spray her. It takes only about five minutes and it makes her incredibly happy. She takes about three baths a week in winter and more in summer.
>
> Doodle, the Parrotlet, takes a bath in her bath dish every day, all year. Our Cockatoo likes fewer baths—maybe once a month in winter, more often in summer. He likes to shower with my husband, but he lets us know if the time is right. When we think it's time, Sherman takes Gandalf to the shower and puts him up on the top of the glass wall. If Gandalf is in the mood, he struts around, talking and laughing. Then when he is ready to get in the water, he spreads his wings and tail and leans down. If he doesn't want a shower, his body language is unmistakable. He holds his wings tight to his body and refuses to come into the shower.

allowed to use the bird clippers. If we nick a bird's vein, I want to reduce the chance that we might introduce bacteria in the wound. You will also need a towel large enough to gently wrap up your bird.

PRACTICE, PRACTICE, PRACTICE

Avoid inflicting pain whenever you can. When you clip the nails, clip as close as you can without trimming into the vein. If your bird has light-colored nails, this is relatively easy and becomes easier with practice. If your bird has dark nails, you cannot see the vein, which makes this operation considerably more difficult. With

Only tiny amounts of the nail need to be removed to keep your bird's nails trimmed.

patience and practice, though, you can learn how far to clip.

Trimming your bird's nails is important. A bird with overgrown nails may catch the nails on loose threads or in small cracks and crevices in her cage. A torn nail is likely to bleed. It doesn't take much for a bird to bleed to death. You may wonder how wild birds survive without regular nail-clipping sessions. Wild birds climb branches, walk on rough stone and land on other uneven surfaces, all of which keeps their nails in trim.

Before you trim the nails, wrap your bird gently in a towel. Avoid making this the only time you wrap your bird in a towel. You can make a game of it on a regular basis, and hug and "tickle" your bird to make it fun. (Finches and Canaries will not enjoy that game.) You will not need a towel to restrain a smaller bird, such as a Cockatiel, a Budgie, a Finch, a Canary or a Pekin Robin. One person can hold one of these birds in one hand, and trim the nails with the other hand.

Although one person can secure a medium-to-large bird and trim her nails, it's much easier with two people. If you clip too deeply and a nail begins to bleed, gather a pinch of cornstarch, flour or styptic powder and press it to the bird's nail. Hold it until the bleeding stops.

Trimming Wings

Trimming wing feathers is easily accomplished with just a few reminders. This really is a two-person operation, at least until you are relaxed and confident about doing it yourself. That will also depend on your bird's reaction to the whole process.

FEATHER-TRIMMING TOOLS

You will need an old, clean towel large enough to wrap up the bird; sharp scissors; cornstarch, flour or styptic powder and a trash bag.

Use of the Towel

I can trim all my birds' wings alone, and so can you. If your bird is afraid of the process, you will need two people. Secure the bird's wings to her body by wrapping the bird in a towel. Larger birds will flap and can hurt you and themselves if not restrained effectively. The towel should not be tight, which might restrict your bird's breathing, nor should it be so loose that the bird can flap freely, however.

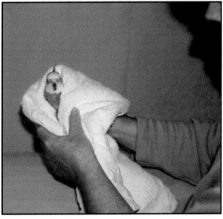

When you have the bird secured, move the towel up on one side, and gently pull out a wing, extending it fully. Examine the wing for blood feathers. Blood feathers still have a blood source. You can easily recognize a blood feather because its quill is semitransparent and the blood shows through. Any feather with a pink or reddish quill is a blood feather. Never clip a blood feather. If you cut a blood feather, your bird can bleed to death unless you pull out the feather immediately, preferably with

If you wrap your bird in a towel, be sure the towel doesn't restrict breathing.

Caring for
Your Bird

needle-nosed pliers. If you cannot do that, you must pack the cut blood feather with cornstarch, flour or styptic powder and apply pressure until the bleeding stops. Have someone call your avian veterinarian immediately.

Provide wood for your bird to chew in order to keep her beak trim.

After you have noted the presence of each blood feather, you can begin to trim. Ideally, you should have observed your avian veterinarian doing this at least once before you begin the task. The number of

feathers to cut will differ, depending on the species of bird. Some lighter-bodied birds need more wing feathers trimmed than do heavier birds. Budgies, Cockatiels and Cockatoos, for instance, are light bodied. Eclectus Parrots are much heavier birds; clipping too many feathers on these birds' wings will make them dangerously clumsy.

Never clip just one wing. This will unbalance the bird. She may still be able to fly, but will have difficulty controlling even a landing. Never clip a bird's tail feathers. These operate as a steering mechanism and help break a fall when she cannot fly.

Many Finches, Canaries and other birds intended primarily as aviary birds need not have their wings clipped. Being fully airborne in their flight cages or aviaries contributes to their sense of well-being. Lovebirds tend to do better with unclipped wings.

If you take your bird to your avian veterinarian or a bird groomer to have her wings and nails clipped, take your own towel, scissors, clippers and styptic powder. This lessens the chance of your bird being exposed to another bird's viruses and bacteria. Too often in those places, as careful as they may be, things get busy and the groomer grabs the nearest towel or tools without making sure they are clean or sterile. You can make sure, though, by bringing your own.

80

Beak Trimming

Beak trimming should never be a concern in a healthy bird. If your bird's beak begins to overgrow, take her to your avian veterinarian for a check-up. Never allow a bird groomer to simply trim the beak as a matter of course. A bird's beak is delicate, living tissue with an active blood source. As such, it has many nerves and is a place of possible contamination with diseases if someone with poor hygiene tries to trim it.

During the course of a healthy bird's life, her beak grows constantly. A healthy bird keeps it the proper length with chewing. Offer plenty of wood of an appropriate size for your bird to play with and destroy. If the beak overgrows and your bird has plenty of opportunity to chew, take her to your vet to find out what has caused the problem. This could be a minor, easily solved problem or it could be a sign of a more serious illness. Get it analyzed right away.

chapter 7

Keeping Your **Bird** Healthy

Keeping your bird healthy should be one of your primary goals. It's really not that difficult to do, if you follow a few guidelines.

Choosing an Avian Veterinarian

Choosing an avian veterinarian may be one of the most important things you do for your bird. This health-care professional can guide you in keeping your bird in top emotional and physical condition; this is the best way to ensure that your companion will live a long, happy life.

THE ASSOCIATION OF AVIAN VETERINARIANS

Not all veterinarians are trained to take care of birds. This is a relatively new specialty and requires extra training not available in all veterinary medical schools. After a veterinarian has taken the extra courses, he or she must be invited to take a qualifying exam. Those who pass this rigorous exam are then qualified and become members of the Association of Avian Veterinarians (AAV).

Membership in this association is important. Those who belong can attend regular conferences where the newest information is shared and quandaries in avian medical care are considered in the hopes of finding answers. In between conferences, avian veterinarians

It is important to find an avian veterinarian who is compassionate as well as highly recommended.

hold other meetings and confer by letter and telephone. This gives you and your bird access to the broadest knowledge base possible.

Once you have established a veterinarian's professional credentials, you must consider the vet's personality. You already know the importance of having a physician who understands and relates well to you and your personality. Perhaps you've also discovered how important it is to have a doctor who listens well and communicates clearly with you. All of these elements should be part of your decision in choosing an avian veterinarian, too.

No matter how technically knowledgeable a caregiver is, if he or she cannot relate to you and your bird in a compassionate, equal-to-equal manner, you should look for another veterinarian. You must have confidence in your veterinarian and be able to understand any directions he or she gives concerning your bird.

POINTS FOR CLEANLINESS

Check the clinic for cleanliness. Ask for a tour. If the veterinarian is at all reluctant to let you see the clinic, you should go elsewhere. Veterinarians are like any other professionals; some are better than others. Those whose clinics are clean and orderly will not prohibit you from taking a look behind the scenes.

WHERE TO LOOK

Finding an avian veterinarian close to your home may be an arduous, but worthwhile process. One of the best ways to begin your search is through a bird club. The members can all give you their advice. Consider it all carefully and if more than one veterinarian has been recommended, interview each one yourself to form your own opinion.

If you don't belong to a bird club, check an annual issue of *Birds USA*, which you can find at most pet stores. In the back is a directory of avian veterinarians. You can also ask regular veterinarians in your area for a recommendation, or call a nearby zoo and ask to speak with the bird curator, who may be able to help.

Ask a veterinarian for the name and phone number of a bird rehabilitator in your area. This person will be another excellent source of information for an avian veterinarian. With the normal cautions, check the Internet for addresses and phone numbers. Don't pass up the chance to work with an avian veterinarian who uses a holistic approach.

Spending lots of time with your bird will help her feel that she is part of a caring flock.

Keeping Your Bird Emotionally Healthy

Keeping a bird healthy involves more than taking her to a good veterinarian. A bird's emotional health is one of the most important keys to her physical health.

Many birds are flock animals. Living in a flock is an advantage for a bird. They help each other hunt for food; some work as a flock to take care of all young; birds preen and feed each other and play together. By living in a group, one bird has a better chance of survival than by living alone. As a group, they can watch for danger. If they fly away in a group, their swift dips and turns may confuse an attacker.

Some species require more affection than others to stay healthy—get to know the typical preferences of your bird's species.

Pet birds maintain those flock instincts. You will become their flock. The more things you do together, the better. This is why it is important to place your bird's cage in a room where you will spend a great deal of time, such as the family room.

MEALTIME

When you eat, put your bird on a stand nearby. Offer some of what you eat, for breakfast, lunch and dinner, so your bird has the feeling that she is eating with you. Do not offer any food that's been in your mouth, though; you have bacteria in your mouth that can make your pet ill. Establish regular times for your bird to get out of his cage. Do this during the first week he is in your home. To a bird, routine is safety and security—as it is to many humans. Try to set up regular times for meals, for bath time and for playtime. If you work away from your home, your bird will adjust to that schedule, too. He just needs to know what will happen

Caring for
Your Bird

at particular times of the day. His internal clock will tell him when it's time for each meal, for you to return and for bed. Occasional changes in the schedule will not hurt, but try to maintain it for the majority of the time.

ESTABLISH A ROUTINE

If you set up the schedule and establish how long, how often and what time your bird will come out of his cage each day, as well as how long he will interact with you, you can avoid many serious emotional problems that could come later. Because a bird can live such a long life, he can become a lifelong companion. You can derive as much pleasure from the relationship as your bird will—if you put time and thought into it.

To learn about how much affection your bird will need to remain healthy, read about his species. If a species generally pairs for life and spends a great deal of each day in social preening, your bird may learn to enjoy

Sindbad, her royal highness, is truly a comeback bird.

gentle hugging with you, cuddling in your lap or next to your neck, as well as petting. A few species of birds sold as pets do not enjoy hugging or petting. Budgies, for example, do not like to be petted, nor do many Lovebirds, Eclectus, Finches or Canaries.

If you buy an older bird that does not seem to like handling, plan to spend years gaining his trust. Your reward may well be a cuddly bird if you don't try to force the issue.

86

SINDBAD'S STORY

When I lived overseas, our vacations were long, so pet owners generally traded care duties. A fellow teacher had an African Grey that I occasionally watched. This bird could not stand well, but was ferocious about not accepting handling. Sindbad learned "Don't you bite me," from my daughter and me. When Sindbad would fall off her perch, we would try to retrieve her, but she seemed to be more interested in biting us than in being helped.

Years later, when her health began to fail, her owners contacted me in the United States to ask if I could find a new owner who could care for her. A dear friend, Julie Rach, took Sindbad, who was in terrible shape physically and emotionally. Today, about ten years later, Sindbad demands that her new owner hold, sere-nade, dance with and cuddle her. This is an amazing turnaround. I would never have predicted it, but then I had no idea of the huge amount of patience and love Julie would give her.

The change is so dramatic that it took me a while to get used to. The first time Sindbad came to stay with me in this country, she looked the same and I was reluc-tant to get close. When she fell off her cage, I had no choice, but the hair stood up on the back of my neck. The change was so complete that she not only cuddles with Julie, but anyone can handle her. Her emotional health is as good as the change in her attitude; she has stopped picking feath-ers, a long-established habit.

If you kiss your bird, restrict it to his upper mandible or the top of his head.

KISSING YOUR BIRD

When you get attached to your bird, you will want to kiss him. I know that be-cause I love kissing my birds.

There is a right way and a wrong way to do this, though. Your saliva contains bacteria dangerous to your bird. For that reason, kiss your bird only on the top or back of his head or the front of his upper mandible with dry lips. If you refrain from kissing any other part of your bird's body, you will help him avoid contact with your saliva when he preens. Never let your bird play with your tongue or teeth, and never let your bird take food out of your mouth.

Birds feed each other. For some bird species, it's a sign of courtship. For others, when chicks are fed by their parents, it is not only a way to get nourishment, it is a way to bond. Your bird may beg for food from your mouth, or he may try to feed you regurgitated food. You can teach him not to engage in these activities by simply distracting him.

Exercising Your Bird

Wild birds fly long distances looking for food each day. When they have chicks, they fly even farther afield. A pet bird has the same need for exercise as a wild bird, and it's up to you to provide the time, the place and the means. Smaller birds should be housed in cages large enough for them to create a good flight path—longer than they are wide, with a perch on each end and no toys or perches in the flight path. Canaries and Finches should be housed in pairs so they have another bird to relate to and interact with. If they are housed properly, they will fly enough to get the exercise they need for good health.

Birds need time out of their cages to stretch their wings and exercise.

Some small and all medium-to-large birds that have clipped wings also need exercise. You can provide this in many ways. Perhaps the simplest is to hold your bird on your arm, raised above your head. Drop your arm a few inches to encourage your bird to flap his wings. If you do this at approximately the same time each day, your bird will learn to take the cue and flap his wings strongly for several minutes, while gripping your arm. With supervision, your bird can also run around on the floor after you have removed all other pets and any children who cannot be trusted with the bird. Most birds will learn to push balls and other toys, another good form of exercise. Ladders and swings also encourage exercise.

You can either buy or make a play gym that hangs from the ceiling. If you make it, be sure to attach some kind of Plexiglas between the chains and the ceiling. This will help to prevent damage. Many birds will climb up and chew the ceiling.

Other play gyms come on stands and are made of manzanita branches or smooth dowels. Buy those made of hardwood. Chewing hardwood can be great exercise for your bird and will keep his mind, as well as his body, occupied. Some of these gyms have swings, ladders, toys and other fun outlets for your bird's energy. It's a good idea to have a play gym that is separate from your bird's cage so you can move it around the house with you.

Signs of Illness

As you look at your bird each day, make it a part of your routine to look for signs of illness. The following can be a guide:

- a bird that sits on the bottom of his cage
- a bird with feathers fluffed for long periods of time
- droopy, dull eyes
- unusual droppings, either in shape, consistency or color
- resting on two feet
- lackluster feathers
- a shiny beak in a Cockatoo
- no interest in preening
- little or no interest in food
- a lack of activity or a lower level of activity

- a change in personality

- a lack of powder of birds that normally have it, such as Cockatoos

- feather picking

- a misshapen or overgrown beak

- lumps on parts of the body that should be smooth

- bleeding or injuries

- convulsions

- vomiting (This is different from regurgitation, where a bird brings up whole food to feed a loved one but otherwise appears healthy. With regurgitation you will notice courtship behavior. If you are unsure, take a sample to your veterinarian.)

- swollen or pasty eyelids

- straining to eliminate

- a swollen vent area (under the tail feathers)

- productive sneezing—a wet sneeze

This list does not cover all possible signs of illness. Your best defense is to watch your bird carefully for abnormal behavior. Your bird cannot talk to your veterinarian to explain his symptoms, or impressions of his illness, but you can watch for signs of illness. Your watchfulness may save your bird's life.

Healthy Behavior

During the first few days your bird is in your home, you will notice a lot of behaviors you are unsure of. Many of these mannerisms are normal for a healthy bird.

- Tail wagging, or flipping, expresses satisfaction with circumstances.

- Dry sneezing, also called unproductive sneezing, removes dust or other detritus from the bird's nasal passages.

- Preening is putting his feathers in order with his beak and tongue.

- Shaking his body after preening helps return all feathers to their normal place.

- Rubbing his beak on his cage bars or perches helps remove food from his beak.

- Chewing his beak, or grinding, as he rests is a sign he is relaxing.

- Yawning may release tension or help him get more oxygen in his system.

- Stretching his wings serves the same purpose as stretching our limbs.

- Chewing at the skin on his foot keeps it in top condition.

- Scratching his head feathers with his foot helps to remove the casings from blood feathers and to put head feathers in the proper place.

- Blinking moistens his eyes and removes foreign objects from his eyes.

This African Grey has nostril drainage, a sign of illness.

Indoor and Outdoor Concerns

Unfortunately, the world is full of hazards for birds, even pet birds. These risks occur both indoors and out. Your best defense for your bird is knowledge. Each room in your home carries with it special problems, but you can effectively reduce the dangers.

HEALTH HAZARDS AROUND YOUR HOME

You may have heard that the home is the most likely place for serious accident for humans, and this is true of birds, too.

Take a look around your home. Remove all nonstick cooking utensils. Move any stained-glass lamps or light catchers that are in nearby windows; remove lead weights from curtains. Lead is toxic to birds.

If your bird shakes his tail feathers, he is probably happy in his home.

Monitor what your bird eats and drinks. Some people still think it's amusing to watch a bird drink alcohol or chew a cigarette. Both can poison the bird, causing his death. If you eat fatty, sugary or salty snacks, do so away from your bird. Instead, share healthful foods such as carrot sticks, apples or other fresh fruits and vegetables—as long as your bird has his food and you have yours.

If you wear costume jewelry, remove it before you go near your bird. Some costume jewelry has lead in it or is colored with lead-based paint. For your own peace of mind, remove any fine jewelry, too. Birds of all sizes are particularly adept at removing or chipping stones or watch stems. Take no chance that your bird might swallow anything of that sort. Shiny objects attract all birds.

Remove any plants that are poisonous to humans. Although we have not tested all plants for toxicity to birds, we should assume that any toxic to children will also harm birds. Replace them with nontoxic plants. All birds will chew on plants, whether they are toxic or not. For this reason, buy only inexpensive plants that you can replace.

The Kitchen

The kitchen is one of the most dangerous rooms in the house for a bird. Some hazards may be a surprise to you, and some of the things I mention may simply remind you of what you already know.

Birds have elaborate and efficient respiratory systems comprised of a system of lungs and air sacs. This is necessary to supply the oxygen needed for flight throughout their systems. While the design of this system is wonderfully efficient for wild birds, it can put pet birds in mortal danger.

Pots, pans, cookie sheets, spoons, spatulas and other kitchen products are coated in plytetrafluoreoetheylene (PTFE), which prevents food from sticking to their surfaces. Used properly, this coating causes no problems, but when it is heated to temperatures of 530° or greater, it can cause birds to die (from polymer fume fever). If your bird is exposed to Teflon toxicity, take him outside to expose him to as much fresh air as possible. Call your avian veterinarian for further instructions. Smoke from kitchen fires not involving PTFE can also kill birds. Additionally, any sprays used in the kitchen, such as oils and insecticides, can be fatal.

Another common problem in kitchens is standing water, whether in a sink or soaking pots and pans. A bird can drown in standing water. When a bird's feathers are wet, his body becomes heavier, making it less likely the bird can fly or flap out of the predicament, even if his wings are not clipped. Also, a bird flying across a column of steam rising from a pan can drop like a rock into a pot of hot food. The damage this accident can do is extensive and your bird might not recover. I take my birds into the kitchen only if nothing is cooking and no one is spraying anything from a pressurized can.

SAFETY FIRST

Many products that we keep in the house are toxic to birds. Your pet will be insatiably curious about anything he encounters. The following products are toxic:

- Dishwasher detergent
- Drain cleaner
- Scouring powder
- Floor cleaner/polish
- Oven cleaner
- Wood polish or wax
- Ammonia
- Ant poison and any other insecticides
- Herbicides
- Metal cleaners
- Pine oil
- Hexachlorophene—present in some soaps
- Matches
- Silver polish
- Window cleaners
- Counter-top cleaners and antibacterials
- Pens
- Marking pens
- Glue
- Bathroom cleaners

Be aware that electric burners can be hot enough to cause severe injury, even when they are not bright red. If you are cooking, put your bird in his cage. Birds have also been known to land on hot oven doors and oven racks, as well as to accidentally fly into open heated ovens.

Food Warnings

Some foods in the kitchen are also a danger to your bird. Keep out of reach anything with chocolate in it. Chocolate contains a chemical called theobromine that is toxic to all pets. Apple seeds contain arsenic, a substance that will build up in a bird's body until it reaches a toxic level. In general, avoid giving your bird fruit seeds and pits because some are toxic, including cherry seeds and apricot pits. Avocado is also reputed to be toxic to birds, although there are conflicting accounts. To be sure, I never allow my birds near it.

If you keep alcohol in the kitchen for cooking, or if you like to have an alcoholic drink as you cook, do not let your bird imbibe. Alcohol poisoning can kill birds. If your bird eats something you believe is poisonous, call your veterinarian or the ASPCA hotline for help. The ASPCA hotline number is (800)548-2423. They will charge you $30 for the consultation.

THE BATHROOM

The bathroom is another area that is inherently dangerous to birds. This does not mean you can never take your bird in the bathroom. If you are aware of the dangers, you can prevent harm to your bird.

The first danger that comes to mind is the toilet. Many birds drown in toilets every year. The solution is so simple: Close the lid on the toilet and train all members of your household to do so as well. Be on the watch for standing water in sinks or the bathtub; a small amount of water can drown a bird. In addition, keep the door to the bathroom closed. The best preventative measure of all is to keep an eye on your bird.

Mirrors pose another hazard in the bathroom. Some birds seem to recognize that the image in a mirror is not a real bird, but others cannot make that distinction. A bird can easily fly into a mirror at full speed, breaking bones, perhaps his neck. After you have gotten to know your bird, you will be able to predict with reasonable certainty whether a mirror in any room is a danger.

OTHER HAZARDS

Other dangers include plants you may have in the bathroom. Birds will chew plants, and many common houseplants are poisonous to birds. Jewelry attracts birds because it is shiny. Aside from the very real damage your pet might do to valuable jewelry, you don't

Closely supervise your bird when he is out of his cage—he may likely decide to explore.

want to let him get in the habit of chewing on jewelry. If you own vintage costume jewelry, stow it away. Older costume jewelry often contains lead, either in the paint or in the adhesive used to hold pieces together. Lead poisoning will kill birds.

Any room in your home contains hazards. The longer you own a bird, the better you will become at spotting dangers.

- Windows can cause trouble in several ways. A window can reflect images much like a mirror, attracting your bird to the bird he thinks he sees there. The best prevention for window problems is to make sure all windows and doors are shut, and that windows are covered with blinds or drapes that let the bird know they are obstacles to flight.

- Increasingly, bedrooms, family rooms, kitchens and living rooms have ceiling fans. Make it a habit to turn off ceiling fans whenever your pet is out of his cage. For absolute safety, consider any fan a potential danger.

- Many plants are toxic to birds. Even if your bird's wings are clipped, he may figure out a way to get to

95

the plants and eat them. The best bet is to remove such plants from your home.

- Aquariums pose another, perhaps unexpected, hazard. These beautiful containers are often placed near walls. A flying bird might crash into the wall and then slide or fall into the aquarium. Once in, the bird will have a difficult time getting out and may drown. Keep a lid on the aquarium.

- Electrical cords can be found in any room of the house, and are a constant danger. Something about these cords attracts birds over and over again. They love to chew them, and therein lies the danger. This is an easily solved problem, though. If you keep cords out of sight, the bird will not be faced with the perilous temptation. If you cannot hide these cords fully with furniture, you can put them in PVC pipes. Run the pipes around any room and up to the electrical outlet.

Remember to close all windows and doors when your bird is out of his cage.

Outdoor Concerns

Most pet birds are slated to live indoors. I strongly recommend this for many reasons, one of the foremost being that you will form a closer bond to a bird that lives in your home than you would have to a bird separated from you by your household walls.

Resist the temptation to bring your bird outside. A pet bird looks like nothing so much as easy prey to predatory birds, such as hawks or falcons. It may also occur to you that it would be fun for your bird to climb in the trees in your yard, but such trees may be toxic to your bird. Sudden gusts of wind have blown birds from shoulders and perches, where they had sat many times before. Recovery efforts are difficult and often fruitless.

Recovering a Lost Bird

While it's difficult to recover a lost bird, it's not impossible. One of the most high-tech ways is to have an encoded microchip placed under your bird's skin. If the bird is captured or found by someone else, the chip can be read to determine who the owners are. You could also have your bird tattooed.

Other methods include taping your bird's calls and playing them loudly outside to attract him to you or to his cage, which is placed away from people, fully stocked with food and treats. The best solution, though, is prevention. Set up regular free-flight times for flighted birds, such as Lovebirds and tame Finches and Canaries.

Make sure all windows and doors are closed before your bird comes out. If your bird is out and on your shoulder all day, teach yourself to double check and put the bird in his cage before you walk out of a door. Know yourself and analyze your situation.

Training

part three

Your Bird

chapter 8

Basic
Training

The most important aspect of training is knowing whether the bird species you have chosen is suited to training. Small birds such as Finches, Canaries and songbirds may be better suited as aviary birds. It is possible to train them to relate to you, but it takes a great deal of time and patience. These birds are not hand-fed because the cost of doing so does not compare well to the price they will fetch on the market. This is true of Budgies, Pekin Robins and Lovebirds, as well. Lower-priced birds are generally not hand-fed.

If you want to train a small songbird, you can do it if you will invest a lot of time. The techniques are the same as for larger birds, except birds with cone-shaped bills do not bite painfully, as hookbills do.

This one fact may give you more confidence than you might have when approaching a hookbilled bird for the first time. You must realize, though, that smaller birds are more easily frightened than larger birds for a number of reasons: They were not hand-fed so they have not learned to trust any human; their size alone causes them to be terrified of any other animal, especially a larger one that could be a potential predator and small birds tend to be highly strung. If you plan to train a small songbird, make a long-range game plan.

Training small birds is possible, but it takes a lot of time and patience.

Training Equipment

Before you begin training your bird, assemble the necessary equipment. You should have on hand a wooden dowel-type perch, an appropriate-size play gym or bird stand and some millet for songbirds; chopped fruit for Lories, Lorikeets, Toucans and Touracos and sunflower seeds or small bits of cheese for Parrots of all sizes.

Some trainers recommend gloves, especially for Parrot training, to protect the trainer from the painful bite a Parrot can inflict. Birds are afraid of gloves, though, and that fear can only make training more difficult, if not impossible, for your bird to feel sure that your intentions are good.

About Bites

Wild birds have few defenses from predators of any sort. They can fly away if possible, and they can bite if

101

*A play gym or
bird stand is a
good place to
start your train-
ing sessions.*

flight is impossible. The extreme pressure a hookbill can exert with her beak to open nuts, bones and other hard food can cause a nasty bite. Toucans and Touracos can also deliver a painful bite when pressed. If a predator grabbed a bird, the bird, in her fright, would bite hard, which could force the attacker to let go.

Until you are a known and trusted part of your bird's life, you represent a possible danger, a mortal danger. Get ready mentally: Your bird may bite you during the training session, but you will gain her confidence more easily if you don't wear gloves. You do have a recourse that will not hurt your bird and will get you out of a painful situation.

If your bird bites you and will not let go, place your thumb and forefinger on opposite sides of her beak, on the skin where the upper mandible meets the lower mandible. Press gently on this area with your fingers. The bird should release you. If she does not, pry her beak apart with two fingers. Put the bird on her perch and begin again. Do not yell or make any sudden moves; this will simply frighten your bird more than she had been, making it likely that you will be bitten again.

Keep in mind, though, that birds use their beaks to steady themselves. When your bird moves from her perch to your arm, she may first grab your arm with her beak. Give her a chance to do so. This is normal behavior for a bird. It may appear as though she is attempting to bite you when she is simply trying to retain her balance.

A Training Room

Choose a room in which you will work with your bird each day. Optimally, it should be small and contain no furniture or knickknacks. I prefer the bathroom for training because it meets these qualifications. If you cannot use the bathroom, choose another room, such as a laundry room, a den or a glassed-in porch, like a Florida room—if you are absolutely sure there is no avenue for escape. A frightened bird—even one with clipped wings—will make valiant efforts to escape, and will find any hole or opening available to do so.

If you have chosen a room with furniture, cover each piece with a drop cloth or blanket, cloak the windows and mirrors and close any doors. If there is a fireplace, close the flue (opening) so the bird cannot fly up the chimney. If you use the bathroom for training, close off the bathtub and shower and shut the toilet lid. Put away any cleaners and tools, such as the toilet brush, which is contaminated with harmful bacteria.

Remove or hide all electric cords. If you will train in a room without carpet, put a blanket or quilt on the floor to cushion the bird's inevitable crash landings. Perhaps the best place to train is inside a stall shower that is large enough for you to sit in. If you choose this option, cover the floor, bring your bird in and close the door. If the door is clear glass, cover it with a sheet so your bird will not try to fly through it. If the door is etched so that it is opaque, you should have no problem. Talk quietly to your bird to gain her confidence before you begin. You can watch her chest for signs of a rapidly beating heart. When the beat begins to slow, your bird has calmed somewhat.

Another great training spot is a bathtub. If your tub is a large Jacuzzi style, you can sit in it with your bird. With her wings clipped, the bird cannot fly out of the tub. Lacking this option, try using a regular-size tub.

You will kneel outside the tub, reaching in to work with your bird. Before you begin work in any tub, cover the bottom with thick towels.

The Main Event: Training Your Bird

Before you begin, remove all of your jewelry and put on clothing you are comfortable in when sitting on the floor. Bring your bird's cage into the training room with a clock, a perch or play gym, a dowel perch and treat seeds. To avoid exhausting the bird—and possibly your patience—the actual working part of the session should not last more than fifteen minutes. Work alone, without other people or animals around.

If you can, play some soft, calming music. If possible, try a new-age tape or tapes of a rain forest, waves or a flowing creek; any of these should help relax you and your bird.

Place the cage on the floor and sit down on the same level several feet away. Talk quietly to your bird, calling her by name and allowing her to get used to her surroundings. When she seems somewhat relaxed, open the door to her cage. Gripping one end of the dowel perch, slide the perch slowly into the cage as you continue to talk to your bird. Keep the long side in front of your bird. The end of the perch could intimidate your pet if you point it at her.

Keep in mind that birds are territorial. Small birds cannot defend their territory and will panic when you put your hands inside the cage. Medium-to-large birds may react by attacking you. Some birds may never allow you to put your hand in their cage, no matter how tame they become or how much they trust you. Other birds may allow certain people this liberty, but not others.

"STEP UP" COMMAND

Put the long side of the perch under the curve of the bird's abdomen, just above her legs. Push up and in (gently but firmly); this will put your bird a bit off balance, forcing her to step up and onto the perch. As you are doing this, say "Step up." When the bird gets on the perch, pull the bird and perch out of the cage to begin the training session. Keep your movements smooth and unhurried. No matter how excited you become over your arrival at this step in the training session, try to appear serene. Do not stare at your bird; this may spark fight-or-flight instincts that serve birds well in the wild. You want to avoid any resemblance to a predator.

If this method does not work, open the cage door and allow the bird to come out on her own. You can tempt her with treats, then sit quietly and wait for her to come out of her cage. Again, avert your gaze and appear disinterested in her actions. As soon as she climbs onto the top of her cage or walks out on her cage door, move slowly toward her with the perch. Next push the perch up under her abdomen to encourage her to step on.

Never grab your bird or use a net. Grabbing will scare your bird and set back the training schedule. Netting a bird can result in injury and panic. Worse, you will lose your bird's trust. Regaining trust will be most difficult and will set back your training schedule for days, perhaps weeks or months.

If the bird jumps off the cage to try to run, let her go. She can only go as far as the limited area in which the two of you are contained. Do not chase the bird. Approach slowly, talking quietly. Begin again with the perch under the bird's abdomen.

Once the bird is on the dowel, move her toward you gradually—at about the level of your face, but lower

> ## QUEEN OF THE CASTLE
>
> Birds are territorial. This instinct helps them survive in the wild. If too many birds try to live in an area, the food will not support the flock or pair. Toward this end, birds will defend their territory however they can—if they can. Larger birds will attack whatever they view as a threat. Small birds will try to get away.
>
> Pet birds retain the same territorial instincts of wild birds. If you put your hand in the cage of a small bird, she will try to get away. The anxiety she will feel as a result of your invasion may stress her immune system, making her more vulnerable to disease. A medium-to-large bird may also panic because she cannot get away from you. Her first reaction may be to attack you to make you go away. You can make a bird fear you by dominating her, but she will not make a good pet, and she may not live long. If your pet is territorial, make allowance for this instinct by keeping your hands out of her cage.

than your eyes, especially if she is a medium-to-large bird. Talk to her gently and in a reassuring manner. If she flutters away, don't chase her with the dowel. Let her sit on the floor until she becomes more calm. Move toward her, still sitting, not standing. Attempt to get her to step up on the dowel again. Say, "Step up." Put the bird on the play gym. Sit nearby, talking to her in a pleasant voice, calling her by name. When the bird seems more composed, encourage her to stand on the dowel again. End the session fifteen to twenty minutes after actual work on the dowel begins.

SUBSEQUENT SESSIONS

During the next session, repeat your actions. After the bird is used to getting on the dowel, it's time to teach her to step onto your hand. To do this, squeeze all fingers together, as you hold your hand in a horizontal

position, thumb tucked tight to the hand. As the bird sits on the dowel or on her play gym, push your hand up under her abdomen. This places the bird off balance, so she will step onto your hand.

This is a big step for a bird. If she bites, try not to react. Certainly you

Stepping onto your hand is a big accomplishment for your bird—it means she is learning trust.

should not withdraw. If you do, you've taught your bird that she can make you go away by biting, and this is a lesson you want to avoid teaching. Prepare yourself for the potential pain of a bite. Your chances of being bitten, though, are greatly lessened if you have taken enough time to gain your bird's confidence. Even training wild-caught birds, I've not been bitten because I watched body language for signs that the bird was not ready to trust me.

If the bird becomes fidgety, pins her eyes, fans her tail or becomes otherwise agitated, return her to her cage.

Talk to her soothingly and return her cage to its normal position in your home. Try again the next day. A one- or two-day delay may be all your new bird needs to see that you mean her no harm. Just as you study your bird, she will watch you to try to determine your motives.

If the bird seems relaxed, you can continue. Talk to her as you work and offer a treat appropriate to her species, such as fruit, cheese, millet or a sunflower seed, if you wish. A little peanut butter on your finger or hand might tempt even the wariest bird. If that's what tempted your pet to step onto your hand, give her time to eat a bit before you continue the session.

SLOW AND STEADY

Always move slowly as you work with your bird. End each session about fifteen minutes after it begins. If your bird was hand-fed and is still young, she will usually tame in a short period of time. It's difficult to predict exactly how long it will take. That can depend on your personality, your bird's personality and experience with other humans, whether she was hand-fed or parent-raised and how young she is.

When your bird will step confidently onto your hand, then you can begin to train her to accept petting and kissing, and then to learn to cuddle. This must all be done in the same unhurried manner as the early training.

SHOULDER PERCHING

Your bird will naturally try to sit on either your shoulder or your head because she will feel more secure when she sits high. This is an instinct. Obviously, you won't want a bird on your head, especially if she's not potty trained. You may begin letting your bird sit on your shoulder, though. You can see her, and she can see you. It seems like a nice way to carry your bird from room to room and to relate to each other in an intimate way. With some birds, this is true.

When you first bring your bird home, do not allow her on your shoulder. Aggressive birds tend to act more belligerent when their eyes are at or above the level of your own. As a general rule, I would not let a medium-to-large bird on my shoulder unless I was sure of her personality, nor would I allow any aggressive bird to sit there.

Quaker Parrots are a good example of a bird that should not sit on a person's shoulder. Some small birds are not suitable for this either; our Parrotlet begins to bite ferociously when he sits on a shoulder. He's only about 2½ inches tall, but he can stretch up and bite earlobes, lips, necks and eyes. If your bird is aggressive, keep her cage top and play gym below your eye level as well.

It's okay to allow some birds on your shoulder, but aggressive birds should be kept at or below your eye level.

PETTING AND HUGGING

If you want to pet your bird, begin by touching her abdomen with one finger. She may bite, but after many sessions, your bird may learn not only to accept this touch, but to welcome it. The amount of touching your bird will accept will also depend on the behavior of her species. If members of that bird's species generally live in flocks, preen each other, feed each other and carry out other close social activities involving touching, she will probably learn to do so with you.

Most smaller birds will remain more fearful of close physical contact and human hands than will larger birds. Individual birds have their own personalities and may react differently than the majority of the members of their species. Each bird is different, just as we are diverse.

Petting her abdomen can be followed by petting her head, but this may be more difficult. Many birds fear having a hand over their backs. If she was hand-fed, though, the breeder gently cupped her head and back in a hand, and she will be used to this position. After your bird accepts petting, you can begin the sometimes slow process of teaching her to cuddle.

TRAINING VARIABLES

If you are working with a young bird, the training sessions will yield the desired results much sooner than if the bird is older or was parent-raised. Such birds are still trainable, but it will simply take more patience and a longer time to accomplish the task. Birds that have been abused present special problems. These birds often can be trained, but you will need to spend a long time gaining the trust of a bird that has seen the worst of human nature—no matter what your intentions.

After your bird is finger-tame, you can work with other members of your household on training sessions. It may be difficult for children to be effective trainers, as they talk loudly and move quickly. However, children are usually eager to make the acquaintance of a new pet. Always supervise interactions between children and birds, for the safety of both.

A bird that was hand-fed will be more likely to accept being held on her back.

Getting Along with Other Pets

If you have other pets in your home, you need to do some serious assessment and training. If you own cats and have brought home a small bird, you may have a problem. Cats naturally prey on birds and they are clever and relentless hunters; small birds are easy quarry. It will become a game for your cat to wait for a time when you are not around to knock down the cage and grab the panicked bird. This is just not a workable mix.

Ferrets, squirrels, snakes or other large reptiles also present a danger to birds. If you own such pets, either find other homes for those pets or do not bring a bird into your home.

If you own a dog, similar precautions are necessary. Large dogs can often be trained to leave a bird alone, either by letting a bird bite her nose or simply by making sure a well-trained dog understands that a bird is off limits. If your dog is poorly trained or high-strung, perhaps you need to rethink your decision to buy a bird other than small ones that will stay safely in an aviary away from the dog.

Acting Up

Discipline is an important part of the relationship between bird and owner, but it must be appropriate. Your bird is a pet; she is not going to carry on your family name or embarrass you in society at large when she grows up.

A few guidelines will help you keep the discipline in perspective. Be prepared to set limits. To set them for your pet, though, you must decide what they are and be consistent. You cannot allow your bird to chew on an old couch cushion, but forbid her to chew your favorite chair. She simply will not understand the difference. Rules must remain simple; a bird will not understand anything complex.

Enforce the rules in a nonviolent way—always. Never hit a bird; that will teach her to react to you in a violent way. Avoid yelling at your bird; it will do nothing beyond encouraging her to make you do it again. Instead, use calm discipline techniques, such as putting your bird in her cage.

If you mainly react to your bird when she misbehaves, you are giving her naughty behavior negative reinforcement. Because she looks for your attention, whether negative or positive, she will repeat the behavior. Instead, offer her praise as well as treats for good behavior, such as playing well with her toys on her cage or eating from her own dish of food as you eat your dinner.

Heavy-handed discipline will not work with birds. Never hit a bird. This will simply make her react to you in fear. The most obvious response to this type of behavior is biting. Yelling will not work either. Birds love drama and loud voices, a red face, arms that pump up and down in excitement all look like fun. Whatever your pet did that caused your reaction will be repeated soon—and often.

SCREAMING

Screaming is an often-cited behavior problem. Many wild birds scream to keep in contact with each other, to alert each other when danger approaches and to express anger, happiness and frustration. They scream to greet the dawn and the dusk. If your bird screams, you must look for the cause. If the bird is frustrated, supply toys—but not in immediate response to the screams. That will only reinforce the behavior. Check to see if your bird has food and water or if she feels

If your bird is screaming, there is probably something causing the behavior.

threatened by another pet or a bird or cat she sees outside. If you made the mistake of giving your bird more attention when she first came home than you do now, establish a regular playtime out of the cage and stick to it. If the bird screams for attention (and is getting adequate attention during the day), ignore the screaming. You want to avoid reinforcing this behavior with any negative or positive reward.

BITING

Biting is another behavior problem common to pet birds. If your bird bites you, do not put her in her cage. She may have bitten you to get away from you. If so, you've rewarded this behavior and the bird will bite

111

again. Instead, suddenly drop the arm on which the bird sits—a few inches for a small bird and perhaps 6 inches for a larger bird. This will put your bird off balance and she will have to stop biting to regain her equilibrium. If she tries to bite again, repeat your action. This is a gentle reaction to your bird's behavior that will cause her to connect biting with the unpleasant feel of being off balance.

Birds misbehave for a variety of reasons. Knowing what they are can help you understand what you may face and allow you to plan your approach. Some birds begin to get more aggressive when they reach sexual maturity. Birds mature at different ages, depending on their species. Your avian veterinarian can help you decide if maturation is causing your bird to act out. In some birds, this causes greater aggression, perhaps biting. Some birds work through this stage, but others will need a mate.

A frightened bird may bite unexpectedly. This is instinctive. A bird afraid for her life has few recourses, and biting is perhaps the most effective. Often people who do not understand birds and their emotional needs frighten birds. Such people cannot seem to resist teasing a bird, and to a bird, teasing is aggressive behavior. She will either respond in fear and withdraw or she will respond with what she perceives as appropriate aggression.

OMINOUS SIGNS

As you get to know your bird, you will begin to recognize threatening behavior. Watching your bird's body language will help prevent injury to you and to your family and guests. Listed here are some of the physical signs of aggression. Not all of them will indicate trouble from your bird; observation is the best way to learn all that you need to know about your pet.

- pulling body feathers tight to her body
- pinning eyes
- fanning tail feathers
- growling
- lifting wings slightly away from her body
- raised crest
- raised foot
- open beak

A sick bird will be more likely to bite or act inappropriately. Compare her feelings to your own when you feel ill. Any bird that has an inadequate diet falls into this category. Emotional problems can also cause bad behavior. If you have established no routine for your

bird, she will feel insecure and may strike out to express that feeling. Your bird needs to be able to predict when her meals will arrive, when she can come out and play and when she will go to bed. Other emotional problems can occur if your family is in a state of uncertainty; during these times your bird will be upset and will act out her feelings.

Introducing Your Bird to Strangers

Introducing your bird to people with whom she is unfamiliar is an important part of your job as leader of the flock. It took you a long time to earn your bird's trust; a misstep could set you back—perhaps permanently. If you have a visitor whom you know will treat your bird badly, do not expose your pet to this person. Whatever teasing you will take is worth protecting your bird from abuse, whether physical or emotional.

Before you have visitors in your home, assess their ability to deal with your pet. If you think they might be rough with your bird or are afraid of birds, either entertain them out of your home, or put your bird in another room where she will be safe.

Some people are afraid of birds. People who suffer from this phobia are terrified of even the smallest birds. Your verbal assurances that your bird is friendly will not ease their alarm. If someone says they don't like or are afraid of birds, leave your pet in her cage. A frightened person may inadvertently injure your bird by dropping or hitting her.

Only introduce your bird to people who respect and like birds.

113

It is also possible that your bird might injure your visitor. An aggressive bird will sense that the visitor is afraid and may become more aggressive than normal, scaring the person further or biting him or her to establish dominance. Because this situation is completely under your control, it's solely your responsibility.

If your visitor seems to be a good candidate for meeting your bird, remember your first sessions with your bird. Take things slowly. This new person must earn your bird's trust, just as you did. Depending on how social your bird is, you may want to simply visit in the room with your bird in her cage. The next time your friend visits, you can let your bird sit with you, choosing whether she will approach your friend. If you continue in this way, your bird will begin a good relationship with your colleague.

chapter 9

Fun
and
Games

Have you ever watched an animal show and wondered how the trainer taught those tricks? Successful trainers watch their animals carefully to learn about their natural behaviors. They then plan tricks that are based on these actions. Killer whales that beach themselves for Sea World shows are repeating behavior they use in the wild to catch seals. Cockatoos that hold out their wings on the verbal cue "Eagle!" are acting out the behavior of wild Cockatoos when they posture for each other.

Trick Training

Using your bird's natural behaviors is the surest way to success if you want to train him to do tricks in response to either verbal or visual cues. If your bird enjoys calling out, you can teach him to answer when you call his name. This training must be done in increments. Call the bird's name. If he makes a noise—any noise—praise him and give him something you know he loves to eat. Keep the treat small so the bird can eat it quickly.

After your bird has made this step, call again and reward only a larger advance, like a louder noise, until you get to the stage you are looking for.

NATURAL BEHAVIORS

If you want your bird to respond to your verbal or visual cues, begin training by utilizing your bird's natural behaviors.

My Eclectus Parrot is not a bird that I would choose to teach tricks. She doesn't have a flamboyant temperament and is not loud. However, Rosebud has learned a small trick. She likes to sit on my arm as I type or write manually. I noticed one night that she bobs her head up and down occasionally. After that, I began to watch for the behavior; the next time she bobbed her head, I nodded mine up and down in an exaggerated way. She studied me curiously the first few times I did it. The first time she responded with a partial head bob, I kissed her on the beak—a reward she enjoys. I continued in this manner, rewarding her for an increasing number of head bobs in response to mine. Now, when I nod my head at her, she responds with a head bob and then cranes her neck up for a kiss on her beak.

Other natural behaviors on which you can base tricks include climbing, picking up shiny objects and putting them in a cup or screaming. If you plan to teach a bird a trick based on an activity unnatural to his species, plan on taking a long time to do it. I taught Gandalf to say "Night, night" when I flip him onto his back. Cockatoos do not normally lie on their backs, although some other species do. It took me a year to teach him to accept the position without biting. It took another six months to teach him to say "Night, night" as soon as I turned him over.

POTTY TRAINING YOUR BIRD

Potty training is probably the best thing you can teach your bird. Once this is accomplished it will be far easier for you to let him out of his cage for long periods of time. Your friends and family will appreciate the trick, too. As soon as they are sure your bird won't soil their clothes, your visitors will want to get to know your bird. You can teach your bird to go back to his cage or to a play gym for this chore. Some birds can be taught to wait until you can put them over a trash can and give the "Go potty" command. In any case, it is not a difficult trick to teach.

Some birds potty train themselves, but don't count on that happening. Part of the training is making yourself aware of how often your bird defecates—about every fifteen to twenty minutes. To train your bird, watch until he defecates in the cage and use the word or phrase you want the bird to associate with the act. In my house, we use "Go potty." Say that when the bird does it spontaneously in the cage, then take your bird out for a play session. In about ten minutes, put the bird back in the cage and wait until he defecates. Say, "Good. Go Potty." The time it will take for your bird to learn the association will vary from pet to pet. In a day or two, you can take the bird out and say, "Go potty." If your bird has made the association, he will do so. If not, keep working.

Some of your bird's more unique habits could be turned into tricks.

TEACHING YOUR BIRD TO TALK

No one should ever buy a bird to teach him to talk; this is a surefire way to disappoint yourself and mistreat a bird by expecting something of him that he may not be able to give. Even among species known to talk, some birds will never utter a word.

If you've chosen a Finch or a songbird, you will not be able to teach him to talk. Although I have heard stories of a few Finches that learned to talk, I haven't heard them myself or seen any evidence that I could trust. My own belief is that these birds cannot talk. A few species,

such as Budgies, African Greys and Amazons, are known to talk, but again, not all birds of these species will learn to do so. Consistently, the bird with the largest vocabulary in various contests is a male Budgie. One had a vocabulary of about 1,000 words.

If you must own a bird that talks and will not be happy with a bird that can't, buy a young bird that already has a vocabulary of a few words. Be prepared to pay more for a bird with this ability.

If your bird's species is one that talks, start training him with simple phrases at a young age.

A great debate has raged among bird keepers and other interested people for years: Do birds that talk mimic, or do they understand what they say and use the words and phrases appropriately? My opinion is that some birds—many birds—learn words and phrases in certain situations, and associate those words with the situation and will then repeat the word or phrase appropriately. Further, studies have shown that some birds can learn to identify objects by name, color, size and shape.

A friend once told me of a wild Amazon Parrot she saw in Mexico. A woman played a scratchy record of "Ave Maria" every day, several times a day. The bird, hanging around in a tree and inside a maze of connected PVC pipes for tidbits each day, learned the whole song. Whenever a man in the house would step outside and call, "Sing my song!" the bird would rise up out of the pipes and sing the whole song, sounds of scratches and other imperfections in the record and all. I'm sure the bird had no idea what the song lyrics meant, but she could mimic a collection of sounds wonderfully. If given the opportunity, though, she might have learned individual words and phrases to which she could relate meanings.

Today, I have two birds that talk. Both birds are of species not known for their talking. My method for teaching them to talk has remained the same. When they are young, I repeat a simple word or phrase to them. If they will talk, they learn the phrase in a few months. After that, the bird generally learns words he hears and can attach some importance to. When Gandalf screams, Rosebud inevitably responds, "Quit that." If Gandalf gets on the floor, Rosebud shouts, "Boy, get back up there." When I call to Rosebud, "Are you all right?" she calls back, "Yeah. Are you all right?" Generally, she's heard Sherman say those phrases under the same circumstances.

In summary, birds can learn to mimic long phrases and songs they cannot possibly understand, but they can also learn words and use them appropriately to request food, ask for a bath or greet you as you come in the door.

"NO SWEAT, JOHN"

Birds can also learn long songs or phrases if they hear them repeatedly. When my husband and I had our first bird, a blue Budgie named John, Sherman said John could never learn to talk. The challenge was on. I'd had a Budgie that talked years before and I was sure John could learn, too. Sherman said he'd only believe it if John could learn to say "No sweat, John." I worked with John for about three months, repeating the phrase over and over whenever we were together.

One day, to my great joy, John said the phrase. Sherman refused to believe it. The next morning, John landed on Sherman's pillow, looked at Sherman and said, "No sweat, John." There can be no doubt that John had no idea what that phrase meant. In just a few days, though, John began to say "Hi!" as he flew to me whenever I walked in the front door. He knew it was a phrase we used when someone came in the door, and that's the only time he used it. Similar phrases followed, often those that were said emphatically.

Playing with Your Bird

Every day, take time to play with your bird. Choose a time when you are relaxed. Play with your bird in ways he will enjoy. If he is a boisterous, confident, hand-fed Macaw, for instance, you can set up a swing and encourage him to swing upside down. If your bird is a bit shy or introverted, perhaps he will simply want to sit in your lap while you read or write. Some birds like to

*As long as you
set aside some
time each day to
play with your
bird, he will be
happy.*

snuggle under a blanket, playing hide-and-seek. Others, such as Budgies, Cockatiels and Lovebirds, like pushing a ball off a counter. While this may not seem too involved, it can be a great deal of fun for you and your bird.

Each bird is different—as different as each owner is from another. It will be up to you to find a common ground. This is another reason to choose a bird that matches your personality. If you are outgoing, choose a bird that is something of an extrovert, such as an Amazon or a Cockatoo. If you are not very outgoing, perhaps a Finch or Parakeet will be best for you.

FUN GAMES

A great game that has a purpose involves a towel. It is invaluable to have trained a pet bird to allow herself to be wrapped in a towel. Once this has been taught, you will find it easy to clip her toenails, to examine her for potential injuries or to let your veterinarian examine her without causing her undue fright.

Instinctively, birds do not like to be contained or trapped. Towels can be terribly frightening to them. To get yours used to a towel, you can begin by playing games with the bird. I prefer to use towels that match my bird's ground color, thinking that they are perhaps more comfortable with those colors. For example, in the case of lovebirds, choose a green similar to their body color. If you do not have a towel this color, choose one that is tan or white. Avoid bright reds and oranges or combinations of those colors with black. These are colors that often mean danger in the wild.

Show the bird the towel in several play sessions. Let your bird climb all over the towel. When the moment seems right, loosely wrap the towel around your bird. Let her climb out at will. As in trick training, take your time. Speed will only panic your bird and delay the training. When your bird allows you to wrap the towel around her body, pet her head and chest gently so she will learn to associate good feelings with the towel. Play peek-a-boo and other little games with the towel. This way, the towel will signify fun to your bird and to you. When it's time to restrain your bird for a more serious purpose, she will not panic.

part four

Beyond
the
Basics

chapter 10

Resources

Books

Athan, Mattie Sue. *Guide to a Well-Behaved Parrot*. Hauppauge: Barron's, 1993.

Athan, Mattie Sue. *Quaker Parakeets*. Hauppauge: Barron's, 1997.

Barber, T.X. *The Human Nature of Birds*. New York: St. Martin's Press, 1993.

Barrie, Anmarie. *Amazon Parrots*. New Jersey: TFH Publications, 1995.

Bedford, Duke of. *Parrots and Parrot-like Birds*. New Jersey: TFH Publications, 1969.

Doane, Bonnie Munro and Thomas Qualkinbush. *My Parrot, My Friend: An Owner's Guide to Parrot Behavior*. New York: Howell Book House, 1994.

Feduccia, Alan. *The Age of Birds*. New Jersey: Harvard University Press, 1980.

Forshaw, Joseph M. Illustrated by William T. Cooper. *Parrots of the World*. New Jersey: TFH Publications, 1978.

Gallerstein, Gary A. *The Complete Bird Owner's Handbook*. New York: Howell Book House, 1994.

Greeson, Linda. *The Charming Little Quaker.* Greeson's Baby Parrots, 1995.

Higdon, Pamela Leis. *The Lovebird: An Owner's Guide to a Happy Healthy Pet.* New York: Howell Book House, 1997.

Higdon, Pamela Leis. *The Quaker Parrot: An Owner's Guide to a Happy Healthy Pet.* New York: Howell Book House, 1998.

Lantermann, Werner. *The New Parrot Handbook.* Hauppauge: Barron's, 1986.

Low, Rosemary. *Parrots: Their Care and Breeding.* London: Blandford Press, 1992.

Lowell, Michele. *Your Pet Bird, A Buyer's Guide.* New York: Henry Holt and Company, 1994.

Murphy, Dr. Joel. *How to Care for Your Pet Bird.* MABH Publishing, 1994.

Parker, Dennis. *Parrots as a Hobby.* New Jersey: TFH Publications, 1994.

Rach, Julie Ann. *The Budgie: An Owner's Guide to a Happy Healthy Pet.* New York: Howell Book House, 1997.

Rach, Julie Ann. *The Cockatiel: An Owner's Guide to a Happy Healthy Pet.* New York: Howell Book House, 1997.

Radford, Elaine. *Step by Step Book about Parrots.* New Jersey: TFH Publications, 1988.

Ruggles, Alison. *Lories & Lorikeets.* London: Blandford Press, 1995.

Schmidt, Horst. *Macaws as a Hobby.* New Jersery: TFH Publications, 1994.

Stunkard, DVM. *A Guide to Diagnosis, Treatment and Husbandry of Caged Birds.* Veterinary Medicine Publishing Company, 1982.

Walker, G.B.R. and Dennis Avon. *Coloured, Type and Song Canaries.* London: Blandford Press, 1993.

Weiner, Jonathan. *The Beak of the Finch*. New York: Alfred A. Knopf, 1994.

Magazines

Bird Talk. Monthly magazine devoted to pet-bird ownership. Back issues or back articles available on request. Subscription information: P.O. Box 57347, Boulder, CO 80322-7347

Birds USA. Annual magazine aimed at first-time bird owners. Look for it in your local pet store or bookstore.

Caged Bird Hobbyist. This magazine for pet-bird owners is published seven times a year. Subscription information: 5400 NW 84 Ave., Miami, FL 33166-3333

Natural Pet. Monthly magazine devoted to the best in natural care for all pets. Available at your local pet or bookstore.

On-line Resources

Bird-specific sites have been cropping up regularly on the Internet. The sites offer pet-bird owners the opportunity to share stories about their pets and trade helpful hints about bird care.

If you belong to an on-line service, look for the pet site (it's sometimes included in more general topics, such as "Hobbies and Interests," or more specifically "Pets"). If you have Internet access, ask your Web browser software to search for "pet birds," or for the specific breed of your bird.

http://nasw.org

http://www.altvetmed.com

Beyond the
Basics

Bird Clubs

The American Federation of Aviculture
P.O. Box 56218
Phoenix, AZ 85079-6128

Avicultural Society of America
P.O. Box 5516
Riverside, CA 92517-5517

International Avicultural Society
P.O. Box 280383
Memphis, TN 38168

Society of Parrot Breeders and Exhibitors
P.O. Box 369
Groton, MA 01450